W9-AYU-961

THE BEDFORD SERIES IN HISTORY AND CULTURE

The Triangle Fire

A Brief History with Documents

Related Titles in
THE BEDFORD SERIES IN HISTORY AND CULTURE
Advisory Editors: Lynn Hunt, *University of California, Los Angeles*
David W. Blight, *Yale University*
Bonnie G. Smith, *Rutgers University*
Natalie Zemon Davis, *Princeton University*
Ernest R. May, *Harvard University*

HOW THE OTHER HALF LIVES *by Jacob A. Riis*
Edited with an Introduction by David Leviatin

Childhood and Child Welfare in the Progressive Era: A Brief History with Documents
James Marten, *Marquette University*

Muckraking: Three Landmark Articles
Edited with an Introduction by Ellen F. Fitzpatrick, *University of New Hampshire*

PLUNKITT OF TAMMANY HALL *by William L. Riordon*
Edited with an Introduction by Terrence J. McDonald, *University of Michigan*

THE JUNGLE *by Upton Sinclair*
Edited with an Introduction by Christopher Phelps, *The Ohio State University at Mansfield*

MULLER V. OREGON: *A Brief History with Documents*
Nancy Woloch, *Barnard College*

TWENTY YEARS AT HULL-HOUSE *by Jane Addams*
Edited with an Introduction by Victoria Bissell Brown, *Grinnell College*

The 1912 Election and the Power of Progressivism: A Brief History with Documents
Brett Flehinger, *California State University, San Bernardino*

OTHER PEOPLE'S MONEY AND HOW THE BANKERS USE IT *by Louis D. Brandeis*
Edited with an Introduction by Melvin I. Urofsky, *Virginia Commonwealth University*

The Sacco and Vanzetti Case: A Brief History with Documents
Michael M. Topp, *University of Texas at El Paso*

THE BEDFORD SERIES IN HISTORY AND CULTURE

The Triangle Fire
A Brief History with Documents

Jo Ann E. Argersinger
Southern Illinois University Carbondale

BEDFORD/ST. MARTIN'S   Boston ♦ New York

For Bedford/St. Martin's

Publisher for History: Mary V. Dougherty
Director of Development for History: Jane Knetzger
Executive Editor: William J. Lombardo
Senior Editor: Heidi L. Hood
Developmental Editor: Shannon Hunt
Editorial Assistants: Katherine Flynn, Jennifer Jovin
Senior Production Supervisor: Nancy J. Myers
Executive Marketing Manager: Jenna Bookin Barry
Text Design: Claire Seng-Niemoeller
Project Management: Books By Design, Inc.
Index: Books By Design, Inc.
Cover Design: Joy Lin
Cover Photo: *Mourners from the Ladies Waist and Dressmakers Union Local 25 and the United Hebrew Trades of New York March in the Streets after the Triangle Fire.* UNITE Archives, Kheel Center, Cornell University, Ithaca, NY 14853-3901.
Composition: TexTech International
Printing and Binding: RR Donnelley & Sons Company

President: Joan E. Feinberg
Editorial Director: Denise B. Wydra
Director of Marketing: Karen R. Soeltz
Director of Editing, Design, and Production: Marcia Cohen
Assistant Director of Editing, Design, and Production: Elise S. Kaiser
Manager, Publishing Services: Emily Berleth

Library of Congress Control Number: 2008933721

For information, write: Bedford/St. Martin's, 75 Arlington Street, Boston, MA 02116   (617-399-4000)

ISBN-10: 0-312-46452-5
ISBN-13: 978-0-312-46452-3

Acknowledgments

Document 10: http://www.ilr.cornell.edu/trianglefire/texts/songs/uprising.html, accessed October 6, 2008. Kheel Center, Cornell University.

Document 18: Reprinted by Permission of the Publisher, Paul S. Eriksson; © 1967 by Rose Schneiderman and Lucy Goldthwaite.

Document 24: From *Up to Now* by Alfred E. Smith, copyright 1929 by the Viking Press, © renewed 1957 by Walter J. Smith. Used by permission of Viking Penguin, a division of Penguin Group (USA) Inc.

Document 25: From *The Roosevelt I Knew* by Frances Perkins, copyright 1946 by Frances Perkins, © renewed 1974 by Susanna W. Coggeshall. Used by permission of Viking Penguin, a division of Penguin Group (USA) Inc.

Foreword

The Bedford Series in History and Culture is designed so that readers can study the past as historians do.

The historian's first task is finding the evidence. Documents, letters, memoirs, interviews, pictures, movies, novels, or poems can provide facts and clues. Then the historian questions and compares the sources. There is more to do than in a courtroom, for hearsay evidence is welcome, and the historian is usually looking for answers beyond act and motive. Different views of an event may be as important as a single verdict. How a story is told may yield as much information as what it says.

Along the way the historian seeks help from other historians and perhaps from specialists in other disciplines. Finally, it is time to write, to decide on an interpretation and how to arrange the evidence for readers.

Each book in this series contains an important historical document or group of documents, each document a witness from the past and open to interpretation in different ways. The documents are combined with some element of historical narrative—an introduction or a biographical essay, for example—that provides students with an analysis of the primary source material and important background information about the world in which it was produced.

Each book in the series focuses on a specific topic within a specific historical period. Each provides a basis for lively thought and discussion about several aspects of the topic and the historian's role. Each is short enough (and inexpensive enough) to be a reasonable one-week assignment in a college course. Whether as classroom or personal reading, each book in the series provides firsthand experience of the challenge—and fun—of discovering, recreating, and interpreting the past.

Lynn Hunt
David W. Blight
Bonnie G. Smith
Natalie Zemon Davis
Ernest R. May

v

Preface

The Triangle factory fire on March 25, 1911, in New York City took the lives of 146 workers—most of them young immigrant women—and became a powerful symbol of the peril industrial workers faced. The tragedy occurred in the wake of the "great uprising" of 1909–1910 among women shirtwaist workers, who had gone on strike for union recognition, higher wages, better treatment from their bosses, and safer workplace conditions. In this period of labor activism and political reform, the fire became a catalyst for significant change. Muckraking journalists depicted the startling contrasts between rich and poor and further exposed the dangers faced by Triangle's workers, stirring both sympathy and outrage among all sectors of the American public and inciting Progressive reformers and factory workers to fight for change.

The Triangle Fire: A Brief History with Documents illuminates the ways in which several distinct forces in the Progressive Era collided, coalesced, and ultimately transformed the political history of a state and a nation. This sensational event, especially when considered alongside the strike that preceded it, illustrates the centrality of women's work to industrializing America and stands as a pivotal moment in the history of American reform. It led to the formation of the New York State Factory Investigating Commission that secured, with remarkable speed, the passage of dozens of laws that enhanced workers' safety and in the process it transformed the Democratic party into a champion of immigrants, laborers, and urban reform. The tragedy, then, forced a reconsideration of the traditional notion of limited government in favor of legislative activism promoting government responsibility and social welfare. Indeed, Frances Perkins, secretary of labor during Franklin Roosevelt's presidency, whose career as a labor reformer was greatly influenced by the Triangle tragedy, declared that March 25, 1911, was "the day the New Deal began."

By weaving together the histories of the Triangle factory workers and the reformers who struggled with them to improve working conditions, the introductory essay in Part One explores the human dimensions of this major industrial disaster while providing background essential for understanding the documents that follow. The first section, "The Garment Industry and Its Workers," focuses on the production of shirtwaists in the Triangle factory and on the work and leisure activities of the "factory girls" in New York City. The second section, "Triangle and the 'Uprising of Twenty Thousand,'" looks at the culmination of labor unrest in the great strike of 1909–1910 and the complicated cross-class alliance between women workers and women reformers. The third section, "The Triangle Tragedy: Grief and Outrage," examines the fire of 1911 and its emotional aftermath, and the final section, "The 'Fire That Lit the Nation': Investigations and Reform," details the arrest and trial of the factory owners and the resulting burst of legislation that helped define Progressive reform in New York and other states.

The contemporary voices throughout the documents in Part Two paint the Triangle story as one of immigration and Americanization, of women's rights and workers' rights, and of machine politics and social justice. The twenty-five documents are arranged in four sections to correspond with the introduction and illustrate the variety of historical sources available and their creative possibilities for study and analysis. These newspaper accounts, personal stories, and songs have been selected specifically for students with an eye for use in a broad range of courses, including women's history, labor history, and the introductory survey of U.S. history. They are meant to help students understand the impact of a major event in a significant era of American history and, most important, to excavate the meanings of diverse and complex stories that collectively represent America's past.

Gloss notes for unfamiliar words and concepts and a chronology of the strike and fire are provided for students' reference. Questions for consideration plus a bibliography with suggested sources and a list of relevant Web sites encourage further analysis of the documents and further exploration of the topic.

A NOTE ON THE TEXT

For the sake of clarity, I have silently corrected typographical errors and misspelled proper names in the document section.

ACKNOWLEDGMENTS

The readers of this manuscript provided thorough and careful critiques that not only enhanced the final version but made it more useful for students and scholars alike. I especially want to thank T. J. Boisseau at the University of Akron; Robert Forrant at the University of Massachusetts Lowell; Andrew E. Kersten at the University of Wisconsin–Green Bay; Glenda Mitchell at the Louisiana School for Math, Science, and the Arts; and Margaret C. Rung at Roosevelt University. My colleague Alan Lessoff at Illinois State University also provided invaluable advice. Barbara Mueller at Southern Illinois University offered important assistance and support. I am particularly grateful for the thoughtful suggestions provided by Kathy Peiss at the University of Pennsylvania. Her own scholarship, moreover, further improved this project.

I have thoroughly enjoyed working with the staff at Bedford/St. Martin's and would like to thank Mary V. Dougherty for her enthusiasm and encouragement for the project. I would also like to acknowledge the support of Heidi Hood, Emily Berleth, Katherine Flynn, Jennifer Jovin, and William J. Lombardo. A special note of gratitude goes to Shannon Hunt, one of the best developmental editors with whom I have ever worked. The book is far better as a result of her splendid skills. In the final stages of production, Nancy Benjamin of Books By Design provided expert assistance.

The person who has contributed most toward this project is my husband and best friend, Peter H. Argersinger. He generously shared his many fine talents as a historian, improving the manuscript in style and substance. It is to him that I dedicate this volume with love.

Jo Ann E. Argersinger

Contents

Foreword   v

Preface   vii

LIST OF ILLUSTRATIONS   XV

PART ONE

Introduction: The Fire That Changed America   1

The Garment Industry and Its Workers   4

Triangle and the "Uprising of Twenty Thousand"   11

The Triangle Tragedy: Grief and Outrage   16

"The Fire That Lit the Nation": Investigations and Reform   26

PART TWO

The Documents   37

1.   **The Garment Industry and Its Workers**   39

    1. Arthur E. McFarlane, *Fire and the Skyscraper: The Problem of Protecting Workers in New York's Tower Factories*, September 1911   39

    2. Pearl Goodman and Elsa Ueland, *The Shirtwaist Trade*, December 1910   43

    3. Rose Cohen, *Out of the Shadow*, 1918   46

4. Sadie Frowne, *The Story of a Sweatshop Girl*,
   September 25, 1902   50

5. Clara Lemlich, *Life in the Shop*, November 26, 1909   56

2.   Triangle and the "Uprising of Twenty Thousand"   58

6. The New York Times, *Arrest Strikers for Being
   Assaulted*, November 5, 1909   58

7 Allan L. Benson, *Women in a Labor War: How the
   Working Girls of New York East Side Have Learned to
   Use Men's Weapons in a Struggle for Better Conditions*,
   April 1910   61

8. The New York Times, *Church to the Aid of Girl
   Strikers*, December 20, 1909   66

9. William Mailly, *The Working Girls' Strike*,
   December 23, 1909   69

10. *The Uprising of the Twenty Thousands (Dedicated to
    the Waistmakers of 1909)*, 1910   71

3.   The Triangle Tragedy: Grief and Outrage   72

11. The New York World, *The Triangle Fire*,
    March 27, 1911   72

12. Chicago Sunday Tribune, *Thrilling Incidents in
    Gotham Holocaust That Wiped Out One Hundred and
    Fifty Lives*, March 28, 1911   76

13. The New York Times, *Partners' Account of the
    Disaster*, March 26, 1911   79

14. Rosey Safran, *The Washington Place Fire*,
    April 20, 1911   84

15. The New York Times, *120,000 Pay Tribute to the Fire
    Victims*, April 6, 1911   87

16. Report of the Red Cross Emergency Relief Committee
    of the Charity Organization of the Society of the City
    of New York, *Emergency Relief after the Washington
    Place Fire: New York, March 25, 1911*, 1912   90

17. Elizabeth Dutcher, *Budgets of the Triangle Fire
    Victims*, September 1912   94

18. Rose Schneiderman, *All for One*, 1967   99

19. Martha Bensley Bruere, *The Triangle Fire*, May 1911   101

4. "The Fire That Lit the Nation": Investigations and Reform   **108**

20. The Outlook, *Indictments in the Asch Fire Case*, April 22, 1911   108

21. The Literary Digest, *147 Dead, Nobody Guilty*, January 6, 1912   110

22. Chicago Daily Tribune, *What the Grave Covers*, September 30, 1913   112

23. State of New York, *Preliminary Report of the Factory Investigating Commission*, 1912   114

24. Alfred E. Smith, *Up to Now: An Autobiography*, 1929   117

25. Frances Perkins, *The Roosevelt I Knew*, 1946   119

APPENDIXES

A Chronology of the Triangle Fire (1900–2001)   122

Questions for Consideration   125

Selected Bibliography   127

Index   131

Illustrations

1. Max Blanck and Isaac Harris, 1911   7

2. Women Shirtwaist Strikers, December 1909   13

3. Fighting the Triangle Fire, March 25, 1911   19

4. Bodies of Vicitims on the Sidewalk, March 25, 1911   21

5. Temporary Morgue on the Twenty-Sixth Street
   Pier, March 1911   22

6. Grieving Friends and Family of the Victims,
   March 1911   23

7. Funeral Procession for the Unidentified Dead,
   April 5, 1911   24

The Triangle Fire

A Brief History with Documents

PART ONE

Introduction: The Fire That Changed America

On Saturday, March 25, 1911, a fire broke out at the Triangle Waist Company in New York City just as the young women workers were leaving for the day. When the foreman rang the closing bell at 4:45, they put away the garments they were stitching and gathered their belongings. Some changed their clothes, donning new spring hats, clutching their pay envelopes, and opening their purses for inspection. Within minutes, however, the discovery of fire on the eighth floor turned their cheerful banter into shrieks of fear and panic, and 180 workers looked desperately for an escape. But the 250 workers on the ninth floor knew nothing of the fire until it engulfed them. Hundreds of firefighters and police raced to the Triangle factory, but young women on the ninth floor had already begun leaping from the window-sills. Fire ladders that could reach only the sixth floor, hoses that reached only the seventh, and nets that broke from the force of the falling bodies proved useless, as did shouts of "Don't jump!" Other workers remained trapped in the roaring flames, and bodies stacked up in front of a locked door. It was nearly midnight before firefighters retrieved all the bodies from the building.

The story of the Triangle fire is one of protest, tragedy, and reform. The site of a labor uprising one year earlier, the Triangle factory became the target of reform in the aftermath of the fire. The story is also about women, mostly young women, their immigrant families and communities, and their roles in industrializing America. And it is about the

Triangle factory, which occupied the top three floors of the Asch Building in New York City. Owned by Max Blanck and Isaac Harris, the Triangle Waist Company produced shirtwaists, or women's blouses, and employed over five hundred workers—predominantly Jewish and Italian women. Blanck and Harris preferred to hire immigrant women, who would work for less pay than men and who, the owners claimed, were less susceptible to labor organization. Moreover, these women were young, poor, and barely educated, and they spoke little English. They lived with their families near the Triangle factory in the Lower East Side—an ethnically mixed but largely Jewish neighborhood that, as one immigrant recalled, served as a hub for the "fascinating interaction of languages and cultures."[1]

Between 1900 and 1920, the forces of industrialization transformed American society with an intensity that shattered traditions and stirred imaginations. Spurred by technological advances, new industries sprang forth, and millions of European immigrants crowded into America's cities, providing the cheap labor that facilitated America's economic transformation. In New York City, many newcomers landed in the garment industry—an industry that doubled in size between 1900 and 1910 and signaled a new America of consumers attentive to style, price, and convenience.

Industrial growth affected factory workers most directly and highlighted such issues as workplace safety, wages and hours, and child labor. Half a million workers suffered injuries, and thirty thousand lost their lives each year. These staggering numbers made the United States the world leader in industrial accidents. Women and children worked for the lowest wages and often in dangerous industries. Sweatshops in the garment industry forced workers to labor in squalid conditions— tiny rooms that were hot in summer and cold in winter and were always noisy, dimly lit, and filled with stoves, irons, sewing machines, and pressing boards. "Sweating" workers—overworking and underpaying them—shocked one observer who decried the "dark, sweltering holes filled with vile odors, hot-beds of disease, rank and foul smelling . . . [and] crowded with perspiring workers."[2]

Sweatshops and slums served as stark reminders of the ills of urban America at the turn of the century. Overcrowded conditions among immigrants at home and at work exacerbated problems of disease and poverty. Responding to these maladies, Progressive reformers attempted to improve the worst conditions of industrial life. A diverse lot, these reformers included men and women, African Americans and whites, religious and political leaders, and muckraking journalists and settlement house workers. They targeted different urban problems and pursued different forms of activism. Some advocated government intervention in order to help immigrants and eliminate slums, sweatshops, and child labor; others called for voluntary organizations and appealed to moral suasion as a primary tactic to combat social problems. Together, however, they worked to expose and eliminate the abuses of industrialization.[3]

Proponents of socialism, although not as numerous as the Progressives, also challenged the inequities of industrial expansion. They dismissed the Progressives' approach as merely ameliorative and called for a more radical transformation of society. Focusing on the conditions under which workers labored and lived, Socialists found a receptive audience among immigrants. In particular, many Eastern European Jews had been exposed to the revolutionary ferment in Russia and brought with them to the United States a strong sense of justice and a political will to struggle for social change.[4]

Progressive and Socialist reformers in New York City confronted a Democratic political machine known as Tammany Hall that resisted substantive reform and relied on traditional boss politics to enrich the machine's coffers and guarantee municipal control. Tammany leaders depended heavily on the political support of Irish Catholics and rewarded loyal voters with jobs, favoritism, and occasional social services. They also attempted to woo such newer immigrants as Italians and Jews, but Tammany's protection of employers at the expense of workers tempered laborers' support. Not only did businesses pay Tammany officials to break strikes and to provide them with lucrative contracts, but the purveyors of urban vice, including gambling and prostitution, received police protection in exchange for their support of the machine. However, New York's Democratic party itself also contained a vociferous group of dissidents who decried bossism and urged the party leadership to become more respectable and civically responsible. Changing the party's structure and political orientation, from either within or without, proved to be a daunting challenge, and the Democratic leadership's preference for politics as usual served to heighten public dissatisfaction.

Women reformers and women workers collectively and independently attempted to improve the lives of wage-earning women in New York's garment industry. Divided by class and ethnicity, they did not always understand each other's positions or priorities. Middle-class reformers often bristled at the class-based critiques of society offered by working women, whereas wage-earning women, especially Jewish immigrants, championed working-class movements, ever skeptical of the middle-class "uplifters," as they called the reformers. Genuine friendships across classes were rare, but these women shared a commitment to social justice and practiced a brand of activism that enhanced women's public role and elevated their political standing. In particular, the Women's Trade Union League (WTUL), established in 1903, brought together an unprecedented coalition of reformers and workers determined to fight oppressive industrial conditions for women workers. By championing labor organization, this diverse collection of women together fought the "tyranny of the foreman" and the antireform policies of Tammany Hall. Their message was simple: All working women, whether native-born or immigrant, deserved respect and recognition at the workplace and in society.[5]

The Triangle shirtwaist factory was one of the WTUL's primary targets. Although it was not a tenement sweatshop but a more modern factory, it still posed daily risks for laborers. The rapid pace of work led to frequent accidents, especially among new sewers who accidentally stitched their fingers instead of cloth. Rows of sewing machines, workers nearly stacked upon each other, and combustible piles of rags and cuttings—all made conditions hazardous and unhealthy. The owners, Blanck and Harris, early earned a reputation for pushing workers to their limits and threatening them against joining a union. The Triangle name elicited ill will among workers even before March 25, 1911. But it was the deadly fire that day at the Triangle factory that symbolized all that was wrong with the new industrial order. The fire was an event of seismic proportions that horrified a city and a nation, refocused national attention, and catalyzed public and political support for industrial reform. A grisly nightmare that took the lives of 146 workers, most of them young women, the Triangle fire came to represent the exploitation of all factory workers and the excesses of unregulated industrial capitalism. It was, indeed, "the fire that changed America."[6]

THE GARMENT INDUSTRY AND ITS WORKERS

Known as the "Shirtwaist Kings," Max Blanck and Isaac Harris were in-laws who presided over the largest shirtwaist factory in New York. Younger and more daring than his partner, Blanck had capitalized on the modest start-up costs in the trade, becoming in 1895 a garment contractor, collecting small bundles of cloth from larger manufacturers and eking out a profit by "sweating" his workers. His success attracted the interest of Harris, and together they formed the Triangle Waist Company in 1900. With a talent for eyeing fashion trends, Blanck and Harris began production of the shirtwaist—a striking innovation in women's clothes that liberated women from the stiff, tight, and frilly Victorian dresses that had nearly immobilized them. Usually made of lightweight cotton or sheer linen, the shirtwaist, or high-necked blouse, became a standard item of dress for women of all classes. Shirtwaists varied in quality and ranged in price from two to several hundred dollars. By allowing more freedom of movement, they suggested a more public role for women, and many women wore shirtwaists and simple A-line skirts to work, to the market, and to church or the synagogue. The demand for shirtwaists skyrocketed, and the Triangle Company expanded, too, providing a moderately priced shirtwaist at $3—a price that was still beyond the reach of many of the workers who produced it.[7]

Blanck and Harris established what was called an "inside shop," where all the steps of production occurred under one roof. Also referred to as "loft" industries, these mechanized factories occupied entire buildings or were located in the upper floors of multistory buildings (Document 1). The building where the Triangle Company was located had been completed in 1901 and was, according to its owner, Joseph Asch, fireproof. Modern in organization and construction, such factories were arranged for maximum productivity and incorporated technological and managerial innovations to boost efficiency and discipline the workforce. The steady improvement of the sewing machine and the cutting knife proved critical to the mass production of shirtwaists. By 1900 mechanically driven sewing machines replaced foot-powered ones and increased the number of stitches per minute from eight hundred to four thousand, allowing the Triangle factory to produce at least a thousand blouses a day.[8]

The Triangle shirtwaists made Blanck and Harris millionaires, and they expanded their operations from one floor to three floors in the Asch Building—numbers eight, nine, and ten. Harris personally designed the arrangement of the 280 sewing machines on the ninth floor to minimize conversation among workers and maximize production. The humming of the sewing machines could be heard fifty-two hours per week, more during peak season. In a complex system, expert cutters carefully placed patterns over one hundred layers of cloth and cut out the shapes, after which supervisors distributed the pieces to a variety of workers who stitched collars, cuffs, and sleeves, leaving the snipping of threads to the youngest girls, who labored for little more than pennies.

The garment industry was a volatile, competitive, and seasonal one that carried all sorts of risks. Over five hundred shirtwaist factories operated in New York City, employing more than forty thousand workers, and competition could be stiff. Fashion trends, moreover, especially in shirtwaists, meant retooling patterns and correctly predicting the styles that would sell. Downturns in the economy adversely affected the sale of clothing, and consumers often postponed purchases when times were hard. Such was the case in New York in 1907, when an economic depression forced Triangle to lay off workers and suspend production for several months. To reduce financial risks, Blanck and Harris relied on the contracting system within their factory. They hired contractors or bosses and paid them a fixed rate for the production of a certain number of shirtwaists. The contractors then hired the workers, mostly immigrant women and girls, and paid them from the amount they received from the owners. Blanck and Harris did not even have a roster of all the employees who worked daily in their factory, preferring to deal only with the contractors. A version of the sweating system, the use of contractors kept down labor costs and distanced Blanck and Harris from their workers. The contractors served as the workers' bosses, and they not only decided on the rates of pay but also closely monitored the work and the workers, for their personal profit depended on minimizing labor costs (Document 2).[9]

As much as they tried, however, Blanck and Harris, like other garment manufacturers, could not completely control the process of production or the behavior of the workers. The threat of labor organization loomed largest in their minds, for they feared that dealing with a union would diminish their profits and their authority over the workplace. The organization of modern factories with large concentrations of workers concerned owners, especially Blanck and Harris, who worried that bonds of solidarity could form among employees, particularly with the aid of union "troublemakers." The garment industry, moreover, was rife with unrest, and tension between workers and management was palpable.[10]

Pauline Newman, later a famous labor activist, began working at the Triangle Waist Company at age twelve. She sat in a corner, dubbed the "kindergarten," with other young girls, snipping threads twelve hours a day. She recalled that the girls sang quietly and secretly told stories to take their minds off the noise, the monotony, and the persistent sniping of foremen, who shouted insults and instructions indiscriminately. A

Max Blanck and Isaac Harris, 1911 Max Blanck and Isaac Harris, known as the "Shirtwaist Kings," established the Triangle Waist Company in 1900. Related by marriage, Blanck and Harris were also neighbors; they lived in luxurious townhouses on the Hudson River and traveled to their factory in chauffeur-driven cars.

Courtesy of the International Ladies Garment Workers Union Archives, Kheel Center, Cornell University.

Jewish immigrant, Newman worked in an industry where Jewish women occupied 60 percent of the jobs by 1911. Italian women formed the next largest group. Together they dominated the workforce in women's clothing — an industry that produced ten times greater volume in New York than in the next largest manufacturing center. Both Italian and Jewish women favored factory work over domestic service, the most common occupation open to women. Despite its hardships, factory work, they believed, was less stigmatized socially and more acceptable culturally. After all, Jewish immigrants had long held a deep respect for the craft of sewing, while Italian families were reluctant to allow their daughters to labor alone in the homes of strangers.

Arriving in the United States in 1901, Newman and her sisters, like many young immigrant women, immediately went to work to support their family. At the Triangle factory, most of the women workers contributed a substantial portion of their earnings to their families in America; others sent money to relatives in Europe (Document 3). They worked to supplement their fathers' meager incomes or assist ailing parents who were unable to endure the long hours of factory work. Daughters, especially in Jewish families, also worked to enable their brothers to attend school. They were, as one observer noted, "married" to their families. They took care of others.[11]

These working "girls," as they were called by their bosses and by themselves, faced challenging conditions on the shop floor. Twelve- to fourteen-hour days were common, and the Triangle owners required them to work on Saturdays, the sabbath for Jewish workers. During the eight months of the peak production season, the work week often included Sundays as well. "When the season was on," Newman explained, "we worked till 9 o'clock," but with "no overtime pay." A sign above the elevator read "If You Don't Come In On Sunday, Don't Come In On Monday." Wages were so low that the seasonality of the industry imposed special hardship on the workers and their families during slack times. They were paid by the piece, and when production was down for several months of the year, they either brought home only a few dollars a week or faced periodic layoffs. "You're laid off. Shift for yourself," a Triangle boss once told Newman. The grueling pace of work further alienated women workers; "the boss is hurrying the life out of me," a woman lamented.[12]

Under constant scrutiny, women workers received fines for talking, singing, and taking too many breaks. "We were like slaves," complained one woman. "You couldn't pick your head up. You couldn't talk. We used to go to the bathroom," but "we hardly had time to wash our hands." The demeaning and petty environment at the factory particularly rankled them. Bosses gave more work to their favorites, and for those less favored, they deducted fines from weekly wages, claiming inferior work. And bosses and foremen routinely teased or insulted the girls while they worked. They made sexual jokes and brushed up too closely to some of the workers, and when women complained, they fined or ridiculed them. Under such circumstances, the bonds of friendship among the working girls took on special meaning. Women relied on each other during the anxious times when bosses and foremen reminded them of their subordinate place on the shop floor.[13]

Still, many women workers also found pleasure in holding jobs, even jobs with long hours and little pay. Although conditions at Triangle "were dreadful," according to Newman, we still "had good times." Away from home and earning money, they traded the confines of parental control for a bit more independence. Newman worked at Triangle for over seven years and cherished the female camaraderie that developed on the shop floor and sustained women at home and at work. As one Triangle worker wrote to Newman, "We shall be friends in joy and sorrow! What is there sweeter in life than the sympathy between woman and woman—what purer than the sincerity of hearts—what greater than the harmony of minds?" Newman warmly agreed, later writing that the bonds forged by women working together meant that "you [were] no longer a stranger and alone." Contemporary observers commented on the spirit and enthusiasm of women garment makers. One street artist who sketched women workers of the Lower East Side described them as "a bevy of boisterous girls with plenty of energy left after a hard day's work."[14]

New York's burgeoning culture of commercialism provided tempting outlets for their energy (Document 4). The excitement of dance halls attracted young women workers, most of them in their teens, and they practiced new steps and "put on style" even after a day's work. Going to the theater was a favorite pastime of New York's wage-earning women, who crowded into variety and vaudeville shows. Excursions to Coney Island were special treats, and the introduction of the movie in nickelodeons led to "nickel madness" among both men and women workers. Even window shopping at the palatial downtown department stores fascinated wage-earning women as they admired the latest fashions. They shared dime novels—adventurous tales of romance, fantasy, and working-class heroines—and traded secrets, clothes, and hats.[15]

Fashion took on special significance for women who labored in the garment industry. Triangle workers absorbed every detail of the shirtwaists they produced, noticing new patterns and the addition of small bits of lace or ribbon or different buttons. Ever conscious of the newest styles, these women workers early learned that clothes signaled both social class and Americanization. Appearance figured prominently in their culture, whether at work or the dance hall. Adorned with what reformer Jane Addams called a "wilderness of feathers," working-class women's hats formed a central staple of garment workers' wardrobes. Although ridiculed by middle-class observers, working women proudly wore their extraordinary "three story hats" to work and to the theater. Indeed, even on the picket line, women workers wore hats to proclaim their respectability and connection to American culture and society (Document 5).[16]

But the sheer press of poverty could limit the participation of women workers in New York's vibrant consumer culture. As one employer explained to a factory inspector, "they're only girls, and girls can't expect to make a lot of money." And they certainly did not. Even after working fifty to sixty hours per week, they did not earn enough to be economically self-sufficient, and those who lived at home were expected to give their earnings to their mothers, receiving in return a small allowance, lunch money, and maybe a little extra for trolley fare to and from work. In 1910 three-quarters to four-fifths of young women workers turned over their unopened pay envelopes to their parents. They routinely skipped lunch and walked to and from the factory in order to save money for clothes and entertainment. They shared expenses and relied on their male friends to treat them to dances and food. Young male workers, after all, not only earned more but also exercised more control over their earnings and were not expected to support the family to the same degree that daughters were.[17]

Long hours of rapid-paced work, especially during the peak production season, sometimes left even the most energetic women without time or strength to enjoy dances, theater, or movies. Parental restrictions further served to limit the social lives of women workers. Both Jewish and Italian daughters were expected to help with housework on their days off, and Italian fathers resisted American ways by insisting on chaperones for daughters who ventured out at night and by denying them permission to attend dance halls and vaudeville shows. Working daughters who embraced American styles and manners often faced the objections of parents, who feared the loss of religious and cultural traditions.[18]

Political activists, particularly Socialist trade unionists among the Jewish immigrants, also questioned the propriety of joining the ranks of Americans in their robust pursuit of the good life. Influenced by labor radicalism, Pauline Newman attempted to educate co-workers at Triangle on the need for reform. She joined the Socialist party at age fifteen and used the shop floor at Triangle as a school for labor organization and social activism. She counseled co-workers against falling into the dream world of dime novels with Prince Charmings and urged them to be more active in the class struggle against industrial capitalism—a system, she explained, that limited their opportunity and denied them respect. Her educational efforts were pointed and occasionally strident, but her Triangle "sisters" still supported and admired her. Moreover, unlike Newman, many of them were able to reconcile their leisure habits with the discipline of union activism. Their militance in the great strike of 1909 offered overwhelming evidence of their twin goals to win respect as "ladies of labor" and to win improved working conditions.

TRIANGLE AND THE "UPRISING OF TWENTY THOUSAND"

The shop floor at Triangle was crowded with cloth and workers and filled with noise from bosses and machines. Clara Lemlich recalled that "the hissing of the machines, the yelling of the foremen made life unbearable." Workers bitterly resented the contracting system that forced them to labor faster and faster—always under the watchful eyes of bosses and even the owners themselves. Blanck and Harris daily walked their factory floors, observing workers whose names they did not know and making sure that no one dawdled. The conditions bred unrest, and workers, who were required to purchase their own needles and thread, saw their meager wages whittled away by excessive charges and punishing fines. They particularly objected to the lack of respect they were shown—marginalized as young immigrant women and daily "searched like thieves" before they left the factory. The bosses treated the "girls," one woman complained, like "the machines they are running. They yell at the girls. They swear at us and sometimes do worse—they call us names that are not pretty to hear."[19]

Dissatisfied with such conditions, over a hundred workers, most of them young women, met secretly one evening in September 1909 to hear representatives of the International Ladies Garment Workers Union (ILGWU) exhort them to take up the cause of the union. Leaders from the WTUL also spoke in favor of the ILGWU. But joining a union could be risky: Loss of employment was usually certain, and the possibility of violence was also real. Clara Lemlich, only five feet tall, worked as an ILGWU labor organizer. Just weeks before the meeting, she suffered a brutal beating from a known gangster rumored to have been hired by her employer.[20]

The morning after the secret gathering, Blanck and Harris, having learned about the meeting from shop-floor spies, issued a stern threat: All workers who joined the union would be fired. But the union activists refused to be intimidated. The Triangle owners promptly dismissed over a hundred workers and shut down the factory. Locked out and with few options, the Triangle workers went on strike. Similar concerns about low wages, poor work conditions, and the lack of respect for workers had already ignited protests at other shops. But the lockout and strike at Triangle captured the attention of the ILGWU, for the company was the largest manufacturer of blouses and its owners were widely regarded as the most ardent anti-unionists among employers. For their part, Blanck and Harris did much to ensure that reputation. They hired prostitutes to act as strikebreakers, accompany newly hired employees across the picket line, and insinuate that the women on strike were streetwalkers themselves. Skirmishes ensued between strikers and strikebreakers, resulting in the arrest of women strikers, who were beaten by police and company guards.[21]

The strike continued for weeks, although some workers returned to their jobs. But the women on the picket line grew more determined, and by November 1909 their smoldering discontent presaged an explosion of protest. Repeated arrests, moreover, attracted the support of middle- and upper-class women, and the WTUL provided financial help and new recruits for the picket line. The front-page arrest of the prominent president of New York's WTUL, Mary Dreier, resulted in the judge's issuing a hasty and apologetic dismissal of the charge (Document 6). This preferential treatment contrasted sharply with the treatment of arrested immigrant women but also generated greater sympathy for the strike and the strikers themselves.

To further publicize the cause, the ILGWU, with the support of the WTUL, urged all workers to attend a general meeting on the evening of November 22. Thousands of workers, most of them women, crowded into the Great Hall of Cooper Union, located four blocks from the Triangle factory. After two hours of speeches, including one by American Federation of Labor president Samuel Gompers, Clara Lemlich sensed the impatience of her co-workers in the audience. Like them, she was disappointed with the cautionary tone struck by the speakers and insisted on speaking on the platform. Raised on a diet of Marxist literature in Russia, Lemlich had arrived in America in 1903 as a young radical. But it was the conditions she experienced in the garment industry that drove her to embrace the ILGWU and call for support for her sister workers. That night she stirred the crowd when she exclaimed: "I have no further patience for talk. . . . I move that we go on a general strike." For five minutes, thunderous applause and cries of support roared through the hall, and all present pledged to go on strike the following day (Document 7).[22]

The next morning the eruption of worker activism stunned the city. Fifteen thousand women garment workers walked off their jobs, and

Women Shirtwaist Strikers, December 1909 Women strikers of the "great uprising" march together to City Hall to protest their harsh treatment on the picket line. Dressed in their best clothes and fashionable hats, these young immigrant women demanded respect from police and public officials alike.

Courtesy of the International Ladies Garment Workers Union Archives, Kheel Center, Cornell University.

another five thousand joined them on day two, culminating in the "Uprising of Twenty Thousand"—the largest single strike by women up until that time. The shirtwaist strikers paralyzed the industry, demanded the recognition of the ILGWU, and called for improved wages and working conditions. Most of all, they wanted respect. Many of them wore banners proclaiming, in Yiddish, "We Are Not Slaves." The general strike served to catalyze a sense of militancy among the "girl strikers." They captured the imagination of the press and the hearts and pocketbooks of upper-class women, who joined forces with the strikers on the picket line, where they were dubbed the "mink brigade" by city newspapers (Document 8).[23]

These middle- and upper-class women embraced the reform tenets of the day. They were true Progressives in their repudiation of what they regarded as the worst abuses of industrialization. They believed workers should have a decent standard of living, and they called on government to right the imbalance of power between employers and workers. They saw their role largely as one of education—arousing the public to demand that political leaders reform labor conditions for wage-earning women. But as women reformers, they held a distinctive vision of reform that also led them to abandon education in favor of the picket line, even risking arrest. Their moral outrage at the treatment of other women fundamentally informed their actions and support. Although they rarely shared the socialist views of the union women they supported, the bonds of womanhood could—and did—foster an alliance of women that added a special dimension to the reform movement of the era.[24]

Despite the joint activism of women reformers and women workers, however, the shirtwaist strikers suffered at the hands of magistrates, hired guards, and city police. Arrested women appeared in court with broken noses and bandaged arms and heads, and the *New York Times* pointed to "torn clothes and bruises" as evidence that the "police mishandle[d] girl strike picketers." But judges refused to acknowledge any brutality and warned the strikers that their gender would not elicit sympathy in the courtrooms. They publicly agreed with factory owners who charged that the picketers had "no respect for the law and no fear of the police" because of "their female sex" and because "they have won the sympathy of wealthy women." Indeed, one magistrate, infuriated by the striking women, told a worker that she was "on strike against God and nature." Another vowed to "do all in my power to stop this disorder." Still another judge challenged the morality of an arrested striker, likening her to a streetwalker and asking "why do you paint your face?"

Annoyed when "charitable women" immediately bailed out the strikers, several judges sent the young women to workhouses rather than imposing fines. Taken to Blackwell's Island, the women were forced to wear prison uniforms and serve five days of hard labor.[25]

The Uprising of Twenty Thousand united women as never before. The first massive strike "run by women and for women," it was, according to one observer, "a 'you-a-girl-and-me-a-girl' spirit that started it." For Clara Lemlich, the general strike represented "a new understanding" among "sister strikers," enabling them to put aside ethnic differences in their common struggle. Margaret Dreier Robins, the national president of the WTUL and sister of New York's WTUL president Mary Dreier, took special pride in the camaraderie that developed between Jewish and Italian women. The Triangle owners, she noted, were known for pitting Jewish and Italian women against each other and for warning parents of Italian daughters against the radical influence of the Jewish working girls. But the strike had served to unify many immigrant women (Document 9).[26]

The uprising also sharpened the sense of justice—and injustice—among the strikers themselves. They became more confident and more aware of their rights and responsibilities. Even as they were carted off to jail, they informed police officers of their legal right to picket. To indicate their contempt for the police and the judges, some paid their exorbitant fines in pennies, clogging the courts and causing great annoyance. The press alternately presented strikers as impoverished waifs and as rowdy girls, but the women themselves resisted such depictions (although they did throw rotten eggs at the Triangle owners and rip buttons off the coats of strikebreakers). Their independence of thought and in dress occasionally even strained their relationship with the socialites who supported them. Middle-class women criticized strikers who wore "gaudy" hats on the picket line, intimidated strikebreakers, or attempted to physically defend themselves from police as "unladylike" and feared that such behavior would diminish public support. But the strikers themselves discounted such concerns and regarded their dress as proper and their actions as courageous. Despite the limits of the newly forged alliance between workers and women of wealth, the mutual support that emerged on the picket line and in the parlor dramatically heightened support for working women and for feminist causes, especially suffrage.[27]

For many, the uprising in New York "marked a turning point in American women's activism," and the contagion spread to other cities. Fifteen thousand women shirtwaist makers in Philadelphia marched off their jobs only weeks after the strike began in New York. Inspired and empowered, other women across the nation followed suit. Over forty thousand garment workers turned out in Chicago. Strikes in the garment industry continued to burst forth with remarkable intensity until 1916, with workers calling for better lives and union recognition. As garment worker and labor activist Rose Schneiderman explained, "The woman worker wants bread but she wants roses, too."[28]

After thirteen weeks and over seven hundred arrests of women workers, more than three hundred New York companies settled with the union, but the Triangle company steadfastly refused. "All of this trouble," Blanck declared, "is over this union business. We did not recognize it and we do not intend to." The Triangle owners did, however, accede to wage increases and shorter hours, but their concessions were not as significant as those made by other employers. The ILGWU and the WTUL called the settlement a victory, and the strike ended in February 1910 (Document 10). Although still supportive of their union, the women who returned to their sewing machines at the Triangle Waist Company knew better. So did the Socialist press, which singled out Triangle for its harsh resistance, adding "With blood this name will be written in the history of the American workers' movement." A little over a year later, the Triangle name would become even more despised as fire destroyed the lives of many of the same women who had fought in the great uprising.[29]

THE TRIANGLE TRAGEDY: GRIEF AND OUTRAGE

On Saturday, March 25, 1911, right before closing time at the Triangle factory, a fire broke out on the eighth floor and quickly spread to the ninth and tenth floors. Its intensity was extraordinary, fueled by piles of clippings, rags, and grease for the sewing machines. Even worse, one of the doors on the ninth floor was locked, trapping workers in a raging inferno. The casualties were high: 146 people dead, all but 23 of whom were women. The youngest victim, Sara Maltese, was only fourteen; her sister and mother also perished in the fire. In one afternoon, Salvatore Maltese lost every female member of his family—his wife and two daughters. The Triangle fire was the deadliest workplace tragedy in the history of New York City—until September 11, 2001—and it occurred in what was billed as a fireproof building.[30]

Probably caused by a cigarette or match tossed into a bin of scraps, the fire started just as workers were lining up for their pay envelopes and opening their purses for inspection—a practice that Blanck and Harris claimed prevented theft and that they required before any woman worker could leave the building. Instantly, a plume of smoke led to cries of "fire!" Several workers began throwing pails of water on the fire; they had done it before when fire had broken out in heaps of cloth. But this time was different—the blaze spread too fast, engulfing a wooden cutting table. Paper patterns and finished shirtwaists hanging from ropes fueled the flames, producing a ball of fire that jumped from table to table and reached the ceiling (Document 11).

No match for pails of water, the fire grew more intense. A worker managed to reach a fire hose in the stairwell, but "it didn't work," as one survivor later explained. "No pressure. No water. I tried it. I turned the nozzle one way and then another. I threw it away." Sheer terror gripped the workers who tried to escape the fire's fury. Panic spread among the 180 people on the eighth floor as workers and bosses pushed toward stairwells and others threw open windows, making their way down a narrow fire escape. Barely able to breathe, workers pressed hard against a locked door until a factory manager produced a key and enabled them to scurry down the stairs. Others rushed the doors of the elevators, and when the cars started to pass the eighth floor en route to the tenth, screaming workers broke the glass window in the door. Their clothing and hair were beginning to burn, and many crowded into the car when it finally stopped. Others were left stranded, desperately waiting for the elevator's return. A relative of the owners managed to alert the tenth floor about the fire before she escaped. But she could not call the ninth floor, for all calls had to go through the switchboard on the tenth, and so no one warned the 250 workers on the ninth floor (Document 12).

Both Blanck and Harris were on the tenth floor, known as the executive floor, along with another fifty people, including pressers, salesmen, and clerical workers. Also present were two of Blanck's daughters, aged twelve and five, who were eagerly awaiting a promised shopping expedition after the close of business that day. As soon as the owners received the warning call, they summoned the elevators, which bypassed the eighth and ninth floors. Twice they filled the cars before deciding that the flames now filling the airshaft made the journey too dangerous, and they escaped to the roof of the building (Document 13). Nearby in another building, a New York University law school professor was lecturing to his class on the tenth floor when the sirens of fire engines, the sight of bellowing smoke and shooting flames, and the chilling screams from women workers on window ledges led him to rush to the roof with his students in tow. Positioning two ladders, they enabled those on the roof of the Triangle Company to escape safely to the law building. All but one from the tenth floor survived.

But the workers on the ninth floor were trapped. Rose Glantz, a ninth-floor survivor, bitterly noted, "We didn't have a chance. The people on the eighth floor must have seen the fire start and grow. The people on the tenth floor got the warning over the telephone. But with us on the ninth, all of a sudden the fire was all around. The flames were coming in through many of the windows." Unable to open a locked door, she found another one but could see only flames: "The fire," she recalled, "was in the hall on the eighth floor. I pulled my scarf tighter around my head and ran right through it. It caught fire. I have a scar on my neck." Many others were not so lucky (Document 14).[31]

The end of the workweek and payday usually provided moments of merriment and frivolity. The girls teased each other, laughed, shared their plans for their day off, and even broke into song, defying the rules of silence that governed their workday. Rose Glantz recalled that she had begun to sing her favorite song, "Every Little Movement Has a Meaning All Its Own," and just as others began to join her, the sight of flames at the windows turned their song into screams.[32]

By design, the arrangement of sewing machines and cutting tables obstructed passageways and limited the movement of workers, and at quitting time each day, workers lined up in a single file for inspection, exiting through the one unlocked door. But on that fateful day, the only unlocked door was filled with flames. Some workers raced to the windows and went down the fire escape. A few went through the open door and up to the roof. Most who escaped were saved by the elevators, which were overflowing with bodies. Facing certain death from the flames all around them, some jumped on top of the elevator cars or slid down the elevator cables. But the scorching heat melted the cables, and many of the remaining workers fled to the window sills. Dozens of women jumped to their death. One horrified firefighter reported, "they pattered on the pavement just like that, just like rain, and we couldn't see them so often as we could hear the thuds."[33]

The fire chief ordered out nets to catch the women as they jumped, but the force of falling bodies ripped apart the nets. "What good were life nets," questioned one firefighter. "The little ones went through life nets, pavement, and all." Even worse, women workers also jumped together, clinging as friends for the last time. Within minutes, the chief abandoned the nets. "When they came down entwined with one another," he sadly noted, "it was impossible [to save them]." Tragedy beget tragedy, and the fire escape, a perilous contraption that ended

Fighting the Triangle Fire, March 25, 1911 Firefighters struggle in vain to reach the fire in the Triangle factory, located on the top three floors of the "fireproof" building. One battalion chief was reduced to merely hoping that a mist from the hoses would "cool off" the workers and prevent them from jumping.

Courtesy of the Franklin D. Roosevelt Library, Hyde Park, New York.

two floors above the ground, began to creak and moan under the weight of bodies pressed together and then collapsed with a terrible cracking noise. The owner of a hat factory watched the collapse in horror. The sounds of death were unbearable; he cried, "I hope I never hear anything like it again."[34]

Assisted by 150 police officers, the fire department was ultimately able to contain the fire within thirty minutes. But it had not been effective during the critical first few minutes: fire hoses could reach only the seventh floor and ladders only the sixth. Firefighters had to climb the stairs with their hoses to contain the mass of flame. To their amazement, the firefighters found the walls and floors intact; indeed, once the fire was extinguished the building looked relatively unscathed. As one reporter noted, the fireproof building showed "hardly any signs of the disaster. . . . [N]othing is the worse for the fire except the furniture and . . . the men and girls that were employed in its upper three stories."[35]

The firefighters then set about the agonizing task of removing the charred bodies from the building, lowering them in bundles to the street level. Onlookers, already stunned by the horror of panicked workers leaping to their death, stood nearly numb as the cleanup of the bodies and debris began. But the crowd grew larger, and desperate families attempted to push through the police line to identify the victims. The wailing sounds of mothers and relatives looking for daughters and siblings could be heard throughout the night.

As ghastly as the Triangle fire had been, the aftermath hardly provided solace to the victims' families. Grief-stricken relatives surrounded the building as police officers counted, tagged, and covered the dead bodies. Some barely able to speak English, anguished mothers tried in vain to find their daughters, but police kept them at bay while the bodies were loaded on horse-drawn carriages and taken to a makeshift morgue set up on one of the city's piers. Other officers collected the belongings that had fallen with the victims: purses, pay envelopes, pieces of scarves and shawls, hair ribbons and combs, and rings, many of them engagement rings. Finally, at midnight, families were allowed to see the bodies in their open coffins. Beginning that night and continuing for four days, the families of victims searched the rows of bodies looking for their loved ones. Some had been burned beyond recognition, and families looked for any clue to help identify them. A brother identified his sister, Mary Goldstein, aged eighteen, by the buttons on her shoes. Ultimately, seven bodies proved unrecognizable, but they were counted in the official death total of 146.[36]

Bodies of Victims on the Sidewalk, March 25, 1911 Helpless onlookers stand amidst the bodies of workers who jumped from the ninth floor of the Triangle factory. Flames and smoke filled the factory as terrified workers struggled to escape, and those who rushed to the window ledge were trapped by a wall of flame inside the building. Police officers and firefighters could only watch in horror as dozens of young women fell to their deaths.
Courtesy of the Franklin D. Roosevelt Library, Hyde Park, New York.

The tragedy had strained every municipal resource—doctors, nurses, police, and firefighters were all called into action. Even the coroner's office had to find additional coffins for all the bodies, and the coroner himself, after visiting the building, left "sobbing like a child." The sight of dozens of young women, hair ablaze, leaping to their deaths shocked the city and the nation and left a lasting impact. Because the fire was such a public spectacle, unlike many industrial accidents, the outpouring of grief and outrage was extraordinary and received daily coverage in papers and magazines. It was, as one poet later wrote, the "day it rained children."[37]

Pauline Newman lost many friends in the fire and fell into a deep depression after the tragedy. Hired by the ILGWU to organize women

Temporary Morgue on the Twenty-Sixth Street Pier, March 1911
Arranged in rows of wooden coffins, the fire victims are housed in a covered
pier pending identification by their families. Identifying badly burned bodies
proved difficult for many relatives. Yetta Goldstein, a leading activist in the
strike against Triangle, was recognized by a cousin only when he saw a gold
button he had given her and a ring with the initials Y.G.
Courtesy of the Hadwin Collection, Kheel Center, Cornell University.

workers, Newman had left for Philadelphia before the fire. Upon hearing of the tragedy, she submitted her resignation to the union, later
explaining, "The Triangle tragedy had a terrible effect on me." Families and friends of the dead grieved publicly and privately, and they
arranged funerals for their loved ones. The families of Sophie Salemi
and Della Costello paid tribute to their special bonds of friendship—
they were neighbors, had worked side by side, and had jumped to their
deaths in a final embrace. Carrying their bodies, two white horse-
drawn hearses led the funeral procession, and dozens of carriages
followed behind. The Lower East Side lost its sounds of hustle and
bustle to the cries of mourners, and the dizzying number of funerals
led to confusion among the processions along the same streets. "This

Grieving Friends and Family of the Victims, March 1911 Women of the Lower East Side grieving for a dead loved one. For days after the fire, sobbing friends and families of the victims filled the streets. The sense of loss that enveloped the city inspired poets and writers then and later to pay tribute to the victims and their families. Morris Rosenfeld, known as the "poet laureate of the sweatshop," published a memorial to the victims shortly after the fire and years later Ruth Rubin penned a ballad of the fire, describing "people weeping bitter tears."
Courtesy of the Hadwin Collection, Kheel Center, Cornell University.

is the funeral of Yetta Goldstein," one sign read. Barely a day went by without a procession; indeed, one funeral director performed eight services simultaneously.[38]

Amidst the grief, the Triangle tragedy unified a city usually divided by ethnic differences and economic tensions. On April 5, 1911, over 350,000 residents turned out in a chilling rain for the funeral of the seven unidentified workers burned beyond recognition (Document 15). Organized by the ILGWU, the massive funeral procession of the nameless victims took on special meaning for the entire city. Municipal officials had refused to release the remains to the union, fearful that

Funeral Procession for the Unidentified Dead, April 5, 1911   Described as one of the most remarkable displays of public grief, the massive funeral procession for the nameless seven victims aroused, observers maintained, a collective sense of guilt for the tragedy and a determination to reform factory life. Courtesy of the International Ladies Garment Workers Union Archives, Kheel Center, Cornell University.

popular unrest would result, and police officers confiscated one thousand copies of an "inflammatory circular" that instructed workers to "Never forgive the enemies of our class." But mostly there was silence as thousands of drenched sympathizers walked for blocks following empty hearses in a display of dignified respect for the fallen. Women of all classes in mud-stained clothes walked arm-in-arm in a captivating show of solidarity. Of special note was the labor activist and WTUL member Rose Schneiderman. According to the *New York Times*, she "brought tears to the eyes of thousands" as she trudged along in the procession "hatless and without raincoat." "Through the east side," the *Times* continued, "where sympathy with the 'silent parade' was most tense, handkerchiefs waved from windows on both sides of the streets." That day, according to the *American*, "was one of [the] most impressive spectacles of sorrow New York has ever known." "This calamity," declared one religious leader, "causes racial lines to be forgotten, for a little while at least, and the whole community rises to one common brotherhood." Others believed the effects of the fire were more permanent: "The Irish cops were picking up the bodies of the Jewish girls and that changed New York politics forever."[39]

The Red Cross and the ILGWU conducted separate relief drives to aid the families and survivors, and the response was overwhelming. Within days, Red Cross officials declined additional donations, saying their organization had received more than enough funds to satisfy community needs. Unlike the union's effort to provide immediate aid to families in need, the Red Cross carefully scrutinized each case and restricted its support for fear that it might lead to dependency (Document 16). But the needs of the families were significant, for in many instances the Triangle victims had been either the sole or the major sources of support for the families. "These girls in their teens," wrote the head of the union's relief committee, "were supporting old fathers and mothers, both in this country and abroad; mothering and supporting younger brothers and sisters, sending brothers to high school, to art school, to dental college, to engineering courses" (Document 17).[40]

Rose Schneiderman worked with both groups, guiding the Red Cross volunteers through the unfamiliar streets of the Lower East Side (Document 18). The volunteers were often unprepared for the stories of sorrow and deprivation they heard. But the fathers and mothers in distant lands were even more shocked when they received money and letters from the Red Cross explaining that their daughters were dead. A Russian blacksmith received about $200 and a letter of condolence from which he learned of his daughter's fate.[41]

Almost immediately, the obvious link between the 1909–1910 Triangle strike and the 1911 Triangle fire triggered public animosity. Observers noted that the Triangle owners had been the most hostile to the union and to the strike and that the owners themselves had been able to escape from the tenth floor by going onto the roof. Women reformers blasted the city's mayor, William Gaynor, for having ignored the pleas of the strikers, adding "Our girls demanded that the overcrowded conditions of that shop be changed." But the mayor, they charged, had "accepted the word of thugs hired by the shirtwaist company" and replied that "he was too busy to bother with us." Clara Lemlich, pointing to the concessions workers were forced to accept to end the strike, declared, "If Triangle had been a union shop there would not have been any locked doors, and the girls would have been on the street almost an hour before the fire started." One reporter, an eyewitness to the fire, acidly affirmed, "I remembered their great strike of last year, in which these girls demanded more sanitary workrooms, and more safety precautions in the shops. These dead bodies told the results."[42]

Three days before the massive funeral procession, a huge crowd turned out to fill the Metropolitan Opera House to capacity. The unprecedented gathering attracted the city's elite and its workers, underscoring broad concerns about the fire and future workplace safety (Document 19). But the configuration of the seating inside suggested that class distinctions were still quite real; the wealthy occupied the orchestra and box seats, and the immigrant workers, fire survivors, and victims' relatives sat in the gallery. Reformers and religious leaders spoke of injustice and the need for change, but the people in the packed galleries booed and hissed at the talk of more committees and more resolutions. Sensing the growing chasm between the demands of workers and the recommendations of city leaders, petite, thin, red-haired Rose Schneiderman rose to speak, her voice barely above a whisper:

> The old inquisition had its rack, its thumbscrews and its instruments of torture with iron teeth. We know what these things are today; the iron teeth are our necessities, the thumbscrews are the high-powered and swift machinery close to which we must work, and the rack is here in the firetrap structures that will destroy us the minute they catch on fire. . . . I can't talk of fellowship to you who are gathered here. Too much blood has been spilled. I know from my experience that it is up to the working people to save themselves. The only way they can save themselves is by a strong working-class movement.

The reaction was electrifying. Even a police officer who had been wary of Schneiderman's politics later commented that "She herself can make you weep. She is the finest speaker I have ever heard."[43]

"THE FIRE THAT LIT THE NATION": INVESTIGATIONS AND REFORM

The disparate voices heard at the Opera House that day agreed on two things: There had to be public accountability for the deaths of 146 people, and factories had to be made safer. But in the immediate aftermath of the fire, responsibility proved elusive. Rather, finger-pointing and confusion prevailed. Mayor Gaynor refused to visit the site of the fire, and Governor John Dix shifted the blame to the city, saying "I find I am powerless to take the initiative in an inquiry." The fire commissioner condemned the Building Department for not enforcing city codes, declaring that the Asch Building was "unsafe to use as a factory." Newspapers further stirred the controversy with political cartoons and editorials that pointed up the absence of local and state leadership. The ILGWU and the WTUL draped the union hall with black sashes, listed the names of the dead, and called for punishment of the guilty. The question would not go away: As the Socialist paper the *Call* asked, "Who is responsible?"[44]

Six different agencies initiated separate investigations of the Triangle tragedy, and their findings further enraged those wanting some measure of justice. Fully half of the city's garment workers, for example, labored above the seventh-floor reach of the fire department's water hoses. Only one hundred of New York's firms were located in fireproof buildings, and the danger of a conflagration even worse than the Triangle fire appeared quite real. Most factories had wooden staircases, inadequate fire escapes, and blocked exits. Investigators found fire escapes shuttered with iron bars; almost all shops were so crowded with workers and machines that an emergency escape would be nearly impossible. In many cases, moreover, workers were not even informed of fire exits, and fire drills were rare occurrences.[45]

Details of the callous indifference of Blanck and Harris to factory safety at the Triangle Company particularly galled the public and angered the victims' families. Several small fires had already occurred in their factory, but dousing with pails of water had minimized the damage. In 1909, in order for Blanck and Harris to receive additional fire coverage, the insurance company had required an inspection, which found that the doors on one side of the building were "usually kept locked" and that many of the workers could barely speak English and needed training on fire drills. Blanck and Harris received the additional coverage but ignored the recommendations.[46]

In 1902 Blanck and Harris had collected nearly $32,000 in damages from their insurer and, after two major fires, had become a high-risk company. They responded by buying larger policies from different companies, and by 1911 they were paying large sums to insure the company for more than its actual value. They received nearly $200,000 from forty-one insurance companies after the Triangle tragedy. Moreover, shortly after the fire, when Blanck and Harris attempted to open a shirtwaist factory at a new loft location, building inspectors fined them for lining up the sewing machines so that "the girls when seated would have no space to move about or leave their places without all getting up together."[47]

A politically astute attorney general, Charles Whitman, early began collecting evidence against Blanck and Harris. He had rushed to the scene of the fire on March 25 and responded favorably to the public's demand for punishment of the owners. Calls for their arrests could be heard on street corners and in mass meetings. Indeed, one reporter confided to a friend, "I would like to hold the rope if there [is] ever any general movement to hang Harris & Blanck." On April 11, Whitman issued his indictments against Blanck and Harris, charging them with first-degree manslaughter in causing the deaths of Margaret Schwartz, age twenty-two, and Rosie Grasso, age sixteen, both of whom were among the "heap of fifty dead bodies discovered by the firemen just back of a closed door on the ninth floor" (Document 20). Whitman maintained that the two partners had knowingly locked the doors, thereby violating the law. "Public policy," he declared, "demands there be no more barred doors, and the manufacturer foolish enough to think he can avoid the law in the future is taking a great risk."[48]

The ensuing trial added more detail and drama to the tragedy. Blanck and Harris were released after each paying $25,000 bail. For their defense, they hired millionaire-lawyer Max Steuer, described by some as the "greatest trial lawyer of our time." Steuer successfully delayed the trial until December 4, when jury selection began. To satisfy the defense, the judge warned jurors against being "affected by any mourning or any weeping in the corridors." But his warning hardly prepared them or the defendants for the following day when a crowd of mothers and sisters of the victims began forming outside the courthouse at eight a.m., waiting for the "murderers" to arrive: "Oh, mamma," shouted one young girl. "Here are the murderers of poor Stella. Hit them, mamma, for killing my poor sister." Three hundred women and girls shouted in unison, "Murderers! murderers! Kill the murderers!" Steuer personally shoved the women away, enabling his clients to escape into the courtroom, but at the noon recess sobbing mothers kissing and waving photographs of their dead daughters lined the corridors and rushed Blanck and Harris once again. Police arrived and cleared the building, but the inconsolable families waited outside the courthouse. At Steuer's insistence, Blanck and Harris were protected by guards for the remainder of the trial, and additional contingents of police kept the protesters in check.[49]

The central issue of the trial was whether Blanck and Harris knew the doors were locked. But the defense focused attention on the "immigrant girls" themselves, who felt the sting of Steuer's insistent questioning as he attempted to discredit them and their testimony. When one woman refused to yield on a specific point, he taunted her about liking to argue, and the judge cautioned her to "answer in a respectful way; just as respectful as you know how," a reprimand that brought tears to her eyes. When another described how she had escaped, Steuer asked, "Was your skirt about as tight as the skirt you've got on now?"[50]

But the chilling testimonies of daring escapes, locked doors, and friends ablaze captured popular attention. For some, the emotional toll of reliving the disaster through their testimony proved debilitating. Lillian Weiner recounted her escape from the ninth floor:

> I ran to the elevator, but it had gone down. I knocked on the door, and it opened, and I fell into the shaft. I fell and fell . . . but something caught on my dress, and I managed to catch hold of the cable. I hung on for all it was worth and slid down. Other persons were falling down the shaft, and one screamed horribly as she passed me. I heard her body crash on the top of the [elevator] cage. Many others fell upon me when I reached it myself. I cannot tell just how I managed to get out alive.

Defense witnesses, some of them relatives of the owners, countered that the doors were unlocked, and Steuer challenged the veracity of the survivors and their relatives, saying "Many of them, because they lost their dearest relatives, are not telling the truth."[51]

The trial lasted more than three weeks, but the jury reached its verdict within one hour and forty-five minutes, finding Blanck and Harris not guilty. The acquittal of the owners devastated families and friends of the 146 victims. Hundreds of mourners waited at the courthouse and shouted and chased after Blanck and Harris, who were hurried away under police escort. The jurors had been unable to find that the partners knew of the locked door and were personally responsible for the deaths of particular individuals, as the judge had instructed. And Steuer had raised doubts about the testimony of the prosecution's key witness, alleging that her account had been scripted by the assistant district attorney. Although the *New York Times* regarded acquittal as the only possible verdict, such other newspapers as the *New York Tribune* called it "one of the disheartening failures of justice which are all too common in this country." The stark headline from the *Literary Digest* simply read "147 Dead, Nobody Guilty" (Document 21).[52]

The not guilty verdict inflamed the public. Families and women workers particularly objected to Steuer's condescending portrait of the factory girls as improper, untutored, and un-American and to the members of the jury who agreed with that depiction. As one juror explained, "I think the factory was well managed and was as good or better than many others. I think that the girls, who undoubtedly have not as much intelligence as others might have in other walks of life, were inclined to fly into a panic." The public outcry intensified when another juror came forward but expressed his regrets for the acquittal of Blanck and Harris, adding that although he did not know whether Harris and Blanck knew the door was locked at the time of the fire, "I could feel sure . . . that the door was locked." The case would not die, and the Triangle name continued to draw anger. In early 1912, at the request of the WTUL, the attorney general issued new indictments against Harris and Blanck, but a few months later they were dismissed on grounds of double jeopardy.[53]

Resentment against the owners flared again in 1913 when Blanck was charged with locking a door at a new shirtwaist factory; this time, he did not deny the charge and was fined $20, the smallest possible punishment (Document 22). In March 1914 Blanck and Harris settled the civil suits that had been filed against them by relatives of the Triangle victims, paying $75 for each life lost three years earlier. The paltry sum stirred more indignation, especially when compared to the amount of insurance the owners had collected, which came to $65,000 more than the losses they suffered in the fire. That same year, Blanck and Harris were fined for sewing fake consumer labels in their garments that falsely indicated they met minimum working standards. Their defense was that their reputation had been destroyed by the fire. Four years later in 1918, the Triangle Waist Company ceased to exist, and Blanck and Harris, shirtwaist kings no more, independently pursued new business ventures.[54]

Frustrated and saddened by what they regarded as legal injustice, workers and reformers were more successful in their efforts to make factories safer. Out of the meeting at the Opera House only days after the fire came a resolution creating the Committee of Safety, which was chaired by prominent attorney and financier Henry Morgenthau. Dissatisfied with political inaction, this committee of leading private citizens launched its own investigation of factory conditions in an effort to expose regulatory inadequacies and push for legislative reform. Significantly, between the women's uprising in 1909 and the Triangle fire, the predominantly male cloakmakers' union led a strike in 1910, which had resulted in a citywide voluntary trade agreement among labor, business, and the public called the Protocol of Peace. Designed to promote industrial stability, the agreement reflected the efforts of several distinguished leaders, all of whom were men. They had not been active in the women's strike of 1909, but after the fire they joined forces with women reformers who had been. Moreover, they knew of the Triangle Waist Company, for it had repudiated the Protocol of Peace, refusing to work with organized labor in any capacity. Several of these men, including Morgenthau, represented the city's financial elite, and their calls for factory reform carried much weight.[55]

The determination of so many prominent women and men to improve factory life combined with the fear of greater activism among workers of all trades to force the political leadership to reconsider its stance toward reform. Key Tammany Hall legislators recognized the need to act. Although motivated by political expedience, party leaders like Alfred Smith and Robert Wagner charted a new course for the Democratic party by embracing factory reform. The party of Tammany Hall on which employers had relied for favors, including the use of police as strikebreakers at the Triangle Waist Company, became the party of industrial reform and worked with its former foes, including Pauline Newman, Clara Lemlich, and Rose Schneiderman.[56]

The reform movement began with the establishment of the Factory Investigating Commission (FIC) by Governor Dix on June 30, 1911. Led by Smith and Wagner, the nine-member commission received broad investigatory power and a charge to propose new laws to protect workers. The scope of authority was unprecedented, and the outcome of the FIC's work was equally unprecedented.

Hired as factory investigators, Newman, Schneiderman, and Lemlich insisted that the political leaders on the FIC receive a taste of the perils of factory work. They demanded, for example, that the FIC members accompany them on unscheduled factory visits. Frances Perkins, the future secretary of labor under Franklin Roosevelt and an eyewitness to the Triangle tragedy, also served as an investigator and aided the effort to educate the commissioners about industrial dangers: "we made sure," she later declared, that "Robert Wagner personally crawled through the tiny hole in the wall that gave exit to a step ladder covered with ice and ending twelve feet from the ground, which was euphemistically labeled 'Fire Escape.'" For Perkins, the fire had been a galvanizing moment that stirred the "public conscience" and produced a collective sense of "public guilt." She was determined to use that moment for all it was worth.[57]

The findings of the FIC were startling. Weekly public hearings exposed in alarming detail the unsafe and unhealthy conditions workers daily faced, and employers and business leaders were unprepared for the extent of the exposure. During the first year of its four-year existence, the FIC inspected over one thousand factories and heard over two hundred witnesses who provided 3,500 pages of testimony

(Document 23). Ultimately producing four volumes described as "masterly analyses of America's new industrial order," the FIC also triggered the passage of over thirty statutes on workplace safety, child labor, and protective legislation for women. "It is true," explained Samuel Gompers, AFL president and member of the FIC, "that at times the community conscience requires a shock to arouse public activity, to secure changes and improvements and reforms. The fire of a few months ago . . . gave an impetus to corrective legislation, as perhaps no one other thing could have done." But to win these reforms, he added, women had "to burn."[58]

With unusual speed and despite intense lobbying of opponents, the New York state legislature passed comprehensive legislation regulating industrial work. Many of the laws became models for other states. They dealt with specific aspects of the Triangle fire, providing more stringent requirements for fire escapes and fire drills and stronger regulations against locked doors, blocked exits and aisles, and the presence of combustible materials. They set new standards for lighting, ventilation, and sanitation and called on employers to protect workers from industrial accidents. They established a new fire prevention bureau and reorganized the state's department of labor, creating a more powerful industrial board to oversee working conditions. And they sought to protect the health and safety of women and children by limiting hours of employment and restricting certain occupations (Document 24). Business leaders denounced the flurry of legislation as an "outcropping of hysteria" and claimed that they had been "paralyzed by an avalanche of so-called remedial laws," but New York had emerged as one of the most progressive states in the nation.[59]

The Triangle tragedy transformed politics and the law. Wagner and Smith were careful not to politicize the reforms they pursued and instead attempted to build new partnerships with labor groups and reformers. By doing so, they helped make Tammany the party of progressive reform rather than the party of cronyism and boss politics. Although the Socialist party remained wary of their reform efforts, as did some old-timers within the Democratic party, they received the support of such groups as the WTUL, the Consumers' League, and the AFL. *The Survey*, a leading journal of social welfare and longtime critic of the Tammany machine, gave the FIC full and favorable coverage, chronicling the efforts of the members and their legislative successes. The FIC effectively constructed a new coalition of political groups and permanently transformed the Democratic party by making it the champion of immigrants, workers, and urban reform. In the legal arena, the fire's consequences were also extraordinary; judicial rulings revised the interpretation of employer liability, challenging the notion of workplace "accidents" and making employers more responsible for the dangers faced by workers on the job. The Triangle fire was, as one scholar noted, a "focusing event" that provoked political reform and created a new public understanding of the hazards of factory life.[60]

Years later, Frances Perkins recalled that she had stood in "frozen horror" as she watched women workers plunge to their death on March 25, 1911, and vowed to ensure that another such tragedy could never occur (Document 25). As secretary of labor under President Franklin Roosevelt, she worked hard to keep her promise, elevating workers' causes and pushing for labor reforms. The ILGWU heralded the tragedy as the "fire that lit the nation" and in 1961, on the fiftieth anniversary of the fire, invited Perkins to pay tribute to the victims. Unveiling a plaque on the corner of the Asch Building, Perkins spoke softly to the crowd, while several Triangle survivors on stage behind her wept silently. The fire, she noted, had been a searing torch of destruction, but from the "ashes of the tragedy" emerged needed reforms that transformed American industrial life. "Out of that terrible episode," she explained, "came a self-examination" throughout America that produced unprecedented legislative change and highlighted the "great human value of every individual." "They did not die in vain," Perkins affirmed, "and we will never forget them."[61]

NOTES

[1]Hasia R. Diner, Jeffrey Shandler, and Beth S. Wenger, eds., *Remembering the Lower East Side: American Jewish Reflections* (Bloomington: Indiana University Press, 2000), 270.

[2]Quoted in Jo Ann E. Argersinger, *Making the Amalgamated: Gender, Ethnicity, and Class in the Baltimore Clothing Industry* (Baltimore: Johns Hopkins University Press, 1999), 14.

[3]Robert F. Wesser, *A Response to Progressivism: The Democratic Party and New York Politics, 1902–1918* (New York: New York University Press, 1986), 21–42; Arthur S. Link and Richard L. McCormick, *Progressivism* (Arlington Heights, Ill.: Harlan Davidson, Inc., 1983), 2–84.

[4]Annelise Orleck, *Common Sense and a Little Fire: Women and Working-Class Politics in the United States, 1900–1965* (Chapel Hill: University of North Carolina Press, 1995), 17–19.

[5]Nancy Schrom Dye, *As Equals and As Sisters: Feminism, the Labor Movement, and the Women's Trade Union League of New York* (Columbia: University of Missouri Press, 1980), 22. For "women's vision" of reform, see Maureen A. Flanagan, *Seeing With Their*

Hearts: Chicago Women and the Vision of the Good City, 1871–1933 (Princeton, N.J.: Princeton University Press, 2002).

[6]The quotation is from David Von Drehle, *Triangle: The Fire That Changed America* (New York: Grove Press, 2003).

[7]Caroline Rennolds Milbank, *New York Fashion: The Evolution of American Style* (New York: Harry N. Abrams, 1989), 33–34, 46–52; Von Drehle, *Triangle*, 46–47; Pearl Goodman and Elsa Ueland, "The Shirtwaist Trade," *The Journal of Political Economy*, 18 (December 1910): 816–18.

[8]Argersinger, *Making the Amalgamated*, 3, 10–11; Leon Stein, *The Triangle Fire* (New York: Cornell University Press, 2001), 22–29; Von Drehle, *Triangle*, 37–39; U.S. Bureau of Labor, *Bulletin*, 183 (Washington, D.C.: 1916), 18–20.

[9]Orleck, *Common Sense*, 15; Stein, *Triangle Fire*, 158–62; Roger Waldinger, "Another Look at the International Ladies' Garment Workers' Union: Women, Industry Structure, and Collective Action," in *Women, Work, and Protest: A Century of U.S. Women's Labor History*, ed. Ruth Milkman (Boston: Routledge & Kegan Paul, 1985), 86–95.

[10]Louis Levine, *The Women's Garment Workers: A History of the International Ladies' Garment Workers' Union* (New York: B. W. Huebsch, 1924), 144–67; Stein, *Triangle Fire*, 163; Richard A. Greenwald, *The Triangle Fire, the Protocols of Peace, and Industrial Democracy in Progressive Era New York* (Philadelphia: Temple University Press, 2005), 30.

[11]Sue Ainslie Clark and Edith Wyatt, *Making Both Ends Meet: The Income and Outlay of New York Working Girls* (New York: The Macmillan Company, 1911), 60.

[12]Elizabeth Ewen, *Immigrant Women in the Land of Dollars: Life and Culture on the Lower East Side, 1890–1925* (New York: Monthly Review Press, 1985), 246–48; Newman quoted in Orleck, *Common Sense*, 36; Triangle boss to Newman quoted in Joan Morrison and Charlotte Fox Zabusky, eds., *American Mosaic: The Immigrant Experience in the Words of Those Who Lived It* (New York: E. P. Dutton, 1980), 10–12; woman worker quoted in Rose Cohen, *Out of the Shadow* (New York: George H. Doran Company, 1918), 113.

[13]Cohen, *Out of the Shadow* 108–14; Ewen, *Immigrant Women*, 248–50.

[14]Orleck, *Common Sense*, 5–7, 35; Morrison and Zabusky, eds., *American Mosaic*, 10; Stein, *Triangle Fire*, vii.

[15]Kathy Peiss, *Cheap Amusements: Working Women and Leisure in Turn-of-the-Century New York* (Philadelphia: Temple University Press, 1986), 88–103, 115–27; Nan Enstad, *Ladies of Labor, Girls of Adventure: Working Women, Popular Culture, and Labor Politics at the Turn of the Twentieth Century* (New York: Columbia University Press, 1999), 48–68.

[16]Enstad, *Ladies of Labor*, 79–80, 66–67.

[17]Argersinger, *Making the Amalgamated*, 86; Peiss, *Cheap Amusements*, 51–54; Enstad, *Ladies of Labor*, 63.

[18]Susan A. Glenn, *Daughters of the Shtetl: Life and Labor in the Immigrant Generation* (Ithaca, N.Y.: Cornell University Press, 1990), 78–89, 137–66; Peiss, *Cheap Amusements*, 67–76.

[19]Lemlich and woman worker quoted in Orleck, *Common Sense*, 33; Von Drehle, *Triangle*, 37; *New York Evening Journal*, 26 Nov. 1909.

[20]Greenwald, *The Triangle Fire*, 30; Alice Henry, *The Trade Union Woman* (New York: Burt Franklin, 1973), 90–91; Von Drehle, *Triangle*, 6–12.

[21]*New York Times*, 5, 6 Nov. 1909; Orleck, *Common Sense*, 58–60, 62; Enstad, *Ladies of Labor*, 91–92; Greenwald, *The Triangle Fire*, 30.

[22]*New York Times*, 5, 14, 23, Nov. 1909; *New York World*, 23 Nov. 1909; *New York Call*, 23 Nov. 1909; Orleck, *Common Sense*, 48–49; Enstad, *Ladies of Labor*, 91–92; Greenwald, *The Triangle Fire*, 32; Glenn, *Daughters of the Shtetl*, 168–69.

[23]*New York Times*, 24 Nov., 2, 20 Dec. 1909; Orleck; *Common Sense*, 61.

[24]For a summary of Progressive reform, see Link and McCormick, *Progressivism*.

[25]*New York Times*, 10, 11, 19, 20, 24 Dec. 1909; 3, 11 Jan. 1910; Enstad, *Ladies of Labor*, 95.

[26]*New York Times*, 16, 19 Dec. 1909; 8 Jan. 1910; Orleck, *Common Sense*, 53; Margaret Dreier Robins to the Editor, *The Survey*, 19 Feb., 1910, 788.

[27]William Mailly, "The Working Girls' Strike," *The Independent*, LXVII (December 23, 1909): 1416–20; *New York Times*, 11, 17 Dec. 1909; 11 Jan. 1910; Enstad, *Ladies of Labor*, 95–123.

[28]Schneiderman quoted in Orleck, *Common Sense*, 6, 57; *New York Times*, 20 Dec. 1909; 16, 24, 25 Jan. 1910.

[29]*New York Times*, 6 Nov. 1909; 8 Mar. 1910; Enstad, *Ladies of Labor*, 160; Stein, *Triangle Fire*, 167–68; Von Drehle, *Triangle*, 86.

[30]This account of the fire is drawn from several newspapers, especially the *New York Times*; Stein, *Triangle Fire*; Von Drehle, *Triangle*; and Greenwald, *The Triangle Fire*.

[31]*Chicago Tribune*, 28 Mar. 1911; *Jewish Daily Forward*, 26 Mar. 1911; *New York Times*, 26, 27 Mar. 1911; Stein, *Triangle Fire*, 30–72; Von Drehle, *Triangle*, 116–70.

[32]Stein, *Triangle Fire*, 54.

[33]*New York Times*, 27, 29 Mar. 1911. For a discussion of the arrangement of the factory floors, see Stein, *Triangle Fire*, 51–61.

[34]*New York Times*, 29 Mar. 1911; Von Drehle, *Triangle*, 148.

[35]Arthur E. McFarlane, "Fire and the Skyscraper: The Problem of Protecting the Workers in New York's Tower Factories," *McClure's Magazine*, XXXVII (September 1911): 467–82; *New York Times*, 26 Mar. 1911.

[36]*New York Times*, 26, 27 Mar. 1911; Von Drehle, *Triangle*, 274.

[37]*New York Times*, 26, 27, 29 Mar. 1911; Stein, *Triangle Fire*, 116–17; Chris Llewellyn, *Fragments from the Fire: The Triangle Shirtwaist Company Fire of March 25, 1911* (New York: Viking Books, 1987), 7.

[38]Orleck, *Common Sense*, 66; Stein, *Triangle Fire*, 147–48.

[39]*New York Times*, 6 Apr. 1911; *The Survey*, 15 Apr. 1911; Stein, *Triangle Fire*, x.

[40]Report of the Red Cross Emergency Relief Committee of the Charity Organization Society of the City of New York, "Emergency Relief after the Washington Place Fire, New York, March 25, 1911" (1912), 5–7, 14, 30, 51; *New York Times*, 1, 12, 16 Apr. 1911; Susan Lehrer, *Origins of Protective Labor Legislation for Women, 1905–1925* (Albany: State University of New York Press, 1987), 150–51; Greenwald, *The Triangle Fire*, 137–38; Elizabeth Dutcher, "Budgets of the Triangle Fire Victims," *Life and Labor*, 2 (September 1912): 265–67.

[41]Stein, *Triangle Fire*, 122–33; Red Cross, "Emergency Relief after the Washington Place Fire," 7, 12, 17, 30.

[42]*New York Times*, 1, 3, 9 Apr. 1911; The *American*, 28 Mar. 1911; Greenwald, *The Triangle Fire*, 132; Martha Bensley Bruere, "The Triangle Fire," *Life and Labor* (May 1911): 137; *Milwaukee Journal*, 27 Mar. 1911.

[43]*New York Times*, 1, 3 Apr. 1911; Orleck, *Common Sense*, 131.

[44]Eric G. Behrens, "The Triangle Shirtwaist Company Fire of 1911: A Lesson in Legislative Manipulation," *Texas Law Review*, 62 (October 1983): 3–12; *New York Times*, 28 Mar.; 1 Apr.; 12 June 1911; Stein, *Triangle Fire*, 113–21; Greenwald, *The Triangle Fire*, 150–52; The *Call*, 31 Mar. 1911.

[45]*New York Times*, 12 June; 2 Apr.; 12 Oct. 1911; State of New York, *Preliminary Report of the Factory Investigating Commission, 1912* (Albany, N.Y.: Argus Company, 1912) II, 620–37 (hereafter referred to as *FIC Report*); McFarlane, "Fire and the Skyscraper," 467–82.

[46]Behrens, "The Triangle Shirtwaist Company," 1–2; Arthur F. McEvoy, "The Triangle Shirtwaist Fire of 1911: Social Change, Industrial Accidents, and the Evolution of Common Sense Causality," *American Bar Foundation Working Paper* #9315 (January 27, 1994): 14–15; Von Drehle, *Triangle*, 160–64; Arthur E. McFarlane, "The Triangle Fire: The Story of a Rotten Risk," *Collier's* (May 17, 1913): 7–8, 28–29.

[47]McFarlane, "The Triangle Fire," 7–8, 28–29; *New York Times*, 18 Oct. 1911; 1 Apr. 1911.

⁴⁸Charles Thompson to "Wm," April 14, 1911, from "The Triangle Factory Fire" Web site, www.ilr.cornell.edu/trianglefire/texts/letters/dearwm_letter.html; *New York Times*, 12 Apr. 1911.

⁴⁹Irving Younger, ed., "Max Steuer's Cross-Examination of Kate Alterman in *People v. Harris*, The Triangle Shirtwaist Company Fire and Max Steuer's & Joseph M. Proskauer's Summations in *Oppenheim v. Metropolitan Street Railways*," Trial Transcript Series, *Classics of the Courtroom* (Minnetonka, Minn.: The Professional Education Group, 1987), foreword; Von Drehle, *Triangle*, 222–23; *New York Times*, 1 Nov.; 5, 6, 7 Dec. 1911.

⁵⁰*New York Times*, 19 Dec. 1911; Stein, *Triangle Fire*, 180.

⁵¹*New York Times*, 9, 12, 13, 14, 15 Dec. 1911; Stein, *Triangle Fire*, 181.

⁵²*New York Times*, 27, 28, 29 Dec. 1911; *Literary Digest*, 6 Jan. 1912. The precise number of the dead was 146, but given the difficulties in identifying the bodies, the numbers initially reported ranged from 141 to 147. A complete list of the victims appears in Von Drehle, *Triangle*, 271–83. See also Stein, *Triangle Fire*, 200–201, and the *New York Times*, 26 Mar. 1911.

⁵³Von Drehle, *Triangle*, 256–58; *New York Times*, 12 Apr.; 22, 29 Dec. 1911, 2 Feb. 1912.

⁵⁴Stein, *Triangle Fire*, 176; *New York Times*, 12 Mar. 1914.

⁵⁵*New York Times*, 3 Apr. 1911; Greenwald, *The Triangle Fire*, 57–93.

⁵⁶Behrens, "The Triangle Shirtwaist Company," 3–12. *New York Times*, 6 Apr.; 9 May 1911; Greenwald, *The Triangle Fire*, 154–88, 219–20; Von Drehle, *Triangle*, 194–218; Thomas M. Henderson, *Tammany Hall and the New Immigrants: The Progressive Years* (New York: Arno Press, 1976), 1–15; Elisabeth Israels Perry, *Belle Moskowitz: Feminine Politics and the Exercise of Power in the Age of Alfred E. Smith* (New York: Oxford University Press, 1987), 82–83.

⁵⁷Orleck, *Common Sense*, 131–34; Frances Perkins, *The Roosevelt I Knew* (New York: The Viking Press, 1946), 17, 22–23.

⁵⁸Gompers quoted in the *FIC Report*, I, 13–26; II, 13; J. Joseph Huthmacher, *Senator Robert F. Wagner and the Rise of Urban Liberalism* (New York: Atheneum, 1968), 5; McEvoy, "The Triangle Shirtwaist Fire," 38, 41, 42. As Alice Kessler-Harris has shown, protective legislation for women also limited their job opportunities and helped ensure their subordinate position in the labor market. See *Out to Work: A History of Wage-Earning Women in the United States* (New York: Oxford University Press, 1982), 180–81.

⁵⁹*FIC Report*, I, 13–26; *New York Times*, 12 June, 12 Oct. 1911; 29 Mar. 1912; 23 Mar. 1913; Lehrer, *Origins of Protective Labor Legislation*, 201.

⁶⁰Greenwald, *The Triangle Fire*, 218–19; Wesser, *A Response to Progressivism*, 71–74; McEvoy, "The Triangle Shirtwaist Fire," 9, 15–18.

⁶¹Bill Severn, *Frances Perkins: A Member of the Cabinet* (New York: Hawthorn Books, 1976), 241–42.

PART TWO

The Documents

1

The Garment Industry and Its Workers

1

ARTHUR E. McFARLANE

Fire and the Skyscraper: The Problem of Protecting Workers in New York's Tower Factories

September 1911

Insurance investigator Arthur McFarlane wrote extensively about the Triangle fire and the owners of the factory. He found, for example, that Max Blanck and Isaac Harris had "overinsured" the factory and, as a result of several fires at the Triangle Waist Company, had become a "rotten risk." Here he discusses the layout of the building and exposes the dangers of production in a loft factory. The report, written several months after the fire, was published in McClure's Magazine—*one of the nation's leading muckraking journals in the Progressive Era.*

New York is the largest factory town in America, but it has no factory district. Its manufactories are disguised behind façades of stone and marble—splendidly lodged in the tallest, most costly and imposing buildings that line Fifth Avenue and Broadway. The great skyscrapers which within the last ten years have shot up like a tropical growth from the famous old residential quarter about lower Fifth Avenue and Washington Square to the great retail shopping district about Twenty-third Street and Madison Square (and on up to the Waldorf

From Arthur E. McFarlane, "Fire and the Skyscraper: The Problem of Protecting Workers in New York's Tower Factories," *McClure's Magazine* XXXVII (September 1911): 466–72.

and above it)—these are New York's factory buildings. They are factories in exactly the same sense as the brick and wooden buildings in Fall River and Lynn. But in this factory district there are no tall chimneys belching smoke, and the pushcart takes the place of the dinner-pail. The buildings in which the factories are housed look like great hotels or office buildings, and the stranger in New York daily comes and goes through the factory district without knowing it. Yet in these splendid skyscrapers there are more factory hands at work than are to be found in Paterson, Lowell, and Fall River all put together.

If you stand at the corner of Fifth Avenue and Twenty-third Street and look south, or stop on Sixth Avenue among the big department-stores and look east or west, your eye will follow, block after block, a succession of great buildings running from twelve to twenty stories in height. Their fronts are of granite, stone, terra-cotta, or ornamental brick, dressed with burnished copper and bronze. The agents' signs upon them describe them as "loft buildings."

A modern loft building is—to gather together several trade definitions—a building from six to twenty stories high, of iron or steel frame, the floors or lofts rising one above another, alike and undivided, for the storing or display of goods. . . . Go up in one of the elevators. While you are still in the car you will begin to hear a low, vicious hum, which, when the elevator door is opened, becomes a snarling roar. You stand bewildered, unable to see what is going on because of the wooden partitions that ramify in every direction. But, if you are allowed access to the "loft" itself, you will find yourself in a single great room, its floor area that of a concert-hall, filled from end to end with men and girls working at motor-driven machines—a hundred, two hundred, five hundred to a floor. You are now in one of New York's factories.

Loft Buildings Never Constructed to Be Factories

Loft buildings were never constructed to be factories, and they first came to be used as such almost by accident. Some fifteen years ago certain garment-makers from the tenements of the East Side and the old dark warehouses of Canal and Grand streets began to look for factories in the regulation sense. The "tenement-made" label was coming, and they wanted cheaper light and power and insurance. But there were no regular factories to be had. They tried the loft buildings, and in these "lofts" they found exactly what they wanted. They got cheaper insurance, because loft buildings were fire-proof. The installation of motors and shafting allowed them to use electricity instead of the old gasoline engines, and electricity was cheaper. There was daylight until five o'clock, even in winter, which meant a saving of gas. Their subcontractors, or sweat masters, could put a quarter more operatives into the same space, and for this reason: The New York factory laws say that every factory worker shall have 250 cubic feet of air. A tenement ceiling is not more than eight feet high; a loft ceiling ten or eleven. And obviously the more space there is above the worker, the less need there legally be around him. Considering the very great amount of floor area always taken up by tables, men and girls and machines could be packed as closely as the chairs could be put and the factory owner still be within the law. There was a saving on every side. . . .

No Fire Department Will Guarantee Fight Fire Successfully Above the Seventh Story

. . . When you permit five hundred workers, four fifths of them women, to be put into a single room one hundred and fifty or two hundred feet above the asphalt, it is necessary to know what you are going to do in case of fire. The most efficient of fire departments will guarantee to fight fire successfully only to a height of eighty-five feet—about that of the seventh story—the height to which water-towers can reach and throw their streams in *levelly*. Streams can be thrown much higher, but they then have no penetrating power. As firemen say, they merely "hit the windows." Chief Croker of the New York department would guarantee to take care of nothing above the seventh story. He said this to every one who would listen to him. But New York did, in the case of her loft factories, what it has become our national habit to do in the matter of danger from fire—decided that there really was no danger, or that, if there were, one could always "take a chance on it." . . .

Loft Factories Not Required to Have Any Fire-Escapes

Regarding fire-escapes themselves the New York building code was non-committal. It did not, apparently, wish to go too far. It said that the above buildings "shall be provided with such good and sufficient means of egress in case of fire as shall be directed by the department of buildings." . . . In the Asch Building, hereafter to be described, it was estimated by the Fire Commissioner that the occupants of the three upper floors could not have got down by the fire-escape in less than three hours. . . .

Passageways to the Exits Are Purposely Made Narrow

When a factory building is not a factory building, it can, manifestly, make no great difference what you put into it. . . . Suppose you visit a loft factory of the most common type—one where waists or white goods are made.

You are stopped at first by the partitions about the doors,—flimsy oak veneer or plain deal board,—turning the crooked alleyways leading to the exits into a kind of labyrinth. If there are two sets of stairways and elevators, you will soon learn that one is set aside, by caste prerogative, for the use of the management and staff. The machine operatives, cutters, and pressers have to use the second. And the partitions generally keep the operatives from knowing that there *is* any but the one exit. When the girls go home at night, they have to pass through a narrow door or down a narrow alleyway of their own, one by one; it is made narrow purposely, so that the watchman outside it can look into their open hand-bags as they pass.

Rooms Crammed with Tissue-Paper, Lace, and Muslin Goods

. . . Box shelving is everywhere, loaded with rolls of flimsy lawn and muslin, cards of lace, and tissue-paper. It would be hard to say what is most inflammable. At the windows hang great bunches of paper patterns. The wooden machine-tables, forty inches wide and stretching from one side of the room to the other, leave at their ends little more aisle space than is needed for the motors and the shafting. The latter is carried to and fro under the table, and, of course, supplies power for the machines. Down the top of the table runs a big wooden trough for the garments to be sewed. And beside every operative stands a large paste-board or pine box, or a wickerwork basket, for the finished garments. Girls do most of the machine work, and they are seated back to back like the "double two" in dominoes; there is so little room in the aisles that their chairs dove-tail. In some factories the high-class garments, when finished, are hung upon lines crossing the room above the heads of the girls. Often gas is used for lighting; and, to get a draft of fresh air through rooms so large, the windows must be kept open. The pressing is done with gas irons; that is, the flame is inside the open iron, within an inch of the goods to be pressed. Some factories do their cutting with an electric knife.

PEARL GOODMAN AND ELSA UELAND

The Shirtwaist Trade

December 1910

During the Progressive Era, reformers, journalists, and academics intensely studied and wrote about the manufacture of garments in factories and sweatshops, focusing on the economics of the industry, the conditions of labor, and the role of technology. In this article, which was part of a larger thesis on the shirtwaist industry, Pearl Goodman and Elsa Ueland capture the volatility of the manufacture of shirtwaists. They studied at the New York School of Philanthropy—founded in 1904 as the first institution of higher education to offer a program in the field of social work.

The shirtwaist trade is a new one, only fifteen or twenty years old, and is also peculiarly local. The great bulk of our shirtwaist manufacture is done in New York and Philadelphia and their suburbs, and the whole country is the market for the waists and dresses made here. But new and local as it is, this shirtwaist industry—or the waist and dress industry, as we might more properly call it, for dresses are made by the same people and in the same shops as waists—has grown to enormous proportions. It does an amount of business in New York City alone which the president of the Associated Waist and Dress Manufacturers estimates is worth a hundred million dollars a year. There are in this city in the neighborhood of 450 factories, employing about 40,000 workers.

The business side of the industry is peculiar and difficult for the very reason that the trade is so new and overgrown and unstandardized. The business may be planned in three ways: "on stock," "on order," or "on contract." The men who work "on order" carry on the bulk of the trade. Their sample makers turn out scores of styles and either their sales agents take these samples about, trying to get orders, or buyers

---

From Pearl Goodman and Elsa Ueland, "The Shirtwaist Trade," *The Journal of Political Economy* 18, no. 10 (December 1910): 816–28.

come to the salesrooms of the factory, see the different styles, and give their orders to the factory. This is a business plan which is apt to demand sudden expansion in the busy season and then to leave the factory in the lurch in the slack season. But it is the plan which involves the least risk from change of fashion and the one most widely adopted. . . .

The trade is full of surprising differences and contrasts in shop organization. One manufacturer has little knowledge of the methods of the next. The first will claim that it is an advantage to have a single skilled girl do as much of the waist as possible, the second will put his shop upon as extreme a "sectional" basis as he can, and make one garment go through thirty hands in the making. Again, in one shop the employees work individually, under the direction of a foreman; in another they work in "partnerships"; in a third they are organized in groups of five or six; in a fourth they are under subcontractors, and in a fifth all these methods may be combined.

There is also unusual diversity of work in a single shop. The tasks range from those performed by a skilled operator to the simple cutting of threads, which can be done by an unpracticed girl of fourteen. Adaptability to change is demanded of the worker in a way that is peculiar to this trade. There may be three or four styles made in a single day. There are various materials prevalent in the various seasons and the workers themselves have to shift sometimes from one kind of work to another.

In one other respect the shops differ widely, and that is in their methods of breaking in the "learners." There is no apprentice system, and yet some of the work requires a great deal of dexterity. How do the girls get started? Some get training by working "partners" with a worker who is more experienced. These partnerships are very common. Often two sisters or two friends will be found who have worked together as partners for years. Only one name or one number is put on the payroll, and the partners divide the wages according to some agreed ratio. . . .

This partnership or group system gives one way of breaking in the "learner"; another way is by subcontracting. The subcontracting system is an admitted evil, a system which has been justly fought by the union. The contractor's interest is to get a quantity of work done by driving employees who have not independence enough to sell their services directly to the boss. The best manufacturers all condemn the system and with one exception [the Triangle Waist Company], there was no subcontracting in any first-class shop. . . .

During the busy season some shops require overtime 1 night a week, some 2, 3, or 4 nights. Of the 100 girls interviewed 72 could give a fairly definite report of their overtime for the past year and the number of nights which these girls worked was estimated as follows:

Overtime Work: Workers' Statement

NUMBER OF NIGHTS IN ONE YEAR	NUMBER OF GIRLS
120 nights	1
From 80 to 90 nights	4
68 nights	1
From 30 to 45 nights	8
From 15 to 29 nights	17
Less than 15 nights	23
None	18
Total	72

... *Seasons.* — From the employers' statements, the average length of the busy season is 9.4 months and of the slack season 2.6 months. The estimate of the workers is somewhat different. The average for the busy season, as calculated from their statements, is 8.5 months, with 3.5 months slack. The average reduction of the force through the slack season was found from the manufacturers' statements to be 42 per cent. . . .

It must be remembered that these weeks of actual idleness have in all cases been preceded by a period of only part-time work, during which wages have fallen very low, and the majority of the workers have been earning very much less than their normal wage. This period is sometimes more trying for a girl than the other, for it means that she goes to the shop and sits perhaps all day, perhaps half a day, without any work to do but simply staying on in the hope that some work may come in during the course of the day. . . .

When high wages do occur in the shirtwaist trade, they are very striking. The great fluctuation in wages is caused largely by variations in the amount of work during the different seasons. But it is also caused by the differences and changes in the price scale that is set by the employer. A price scale has to be adjusted for every operation that is done by the piece, and it has to be changed with the different styles made and the different materials that are used. . . . A waist that a factory hand sews for 20 cents retails for about $3.75; a 60-cent waist retails for as much as $15.00.

Manufacturers differ a great deal in their schemes for setting the price scale. Nearly all of them will admit that they sometimes make mistakes in setting the rate. . . .

The investigation showed, then, long hours, a great deal of overtime work, sharp fluctuations in wages owing to the seasonal character of the work and the shifting price scales, and a complete lack of any standards as to wages or methods of business among the manufacturers.

3

ROSE COHEN

Out of the Shadow

1918

Born in a small Russian village, Rose Cohen lived with her mother, father, four siblings, and grandparents in a log house with a straw roof. A victim of anti-Semitism, her father fled to America, found work as a tailor, and saved enough money to send for his eldest daughter. In his letter, he explained that Rose could earn at least three dollars per week in America, adding "with her help, I'll be able to bring the rest of the family over sooner, perhaps in a year or so." She joined her father in New York City at age twelve and shortly thereafter took her first job in a sweatshop, which her father had arranged for her.

A survivor of the Triangle fire, Cohen writes of her loneliness and her first work experience.

Father began to strain all his energy to save the money to send for mother and the children. In the shop one morning I realised that he had been leaving out of his breakfast the tiny glass of brandy for two cents and was eating just the roll. So I too made my sacrifice. When as usual he gave me the apple and the roll, I took the roll but refused the apple. And he did not urge me. When a cold grey day at the end of

From Rose Cohen, *Out of the Shadow: A Russian Jewish Girlhood on the Lower East Side* (New York: George H. Doran Company, 1918), 108–14.

November found him in his light tan suit quite worn and me in my thin calico frock, now washed out to a tan colour, we went to a second-hand clothing store on Division Street and he bought me a fuzzy brown coat reaching a little below my waist, for fifty cents, and for himself a thin threadbare overcoat. And now we were ready for the winter.

About the same time that the bitter cold came father told me one night that he had found work for me in a shop where he knew the presser. I lay awake long that night. I was eager to begin life on my own responsibility but was also afraid. We rose earlier than usual that morning for father had to take me to the shop and not be over late for his own work. I wrapped my thimble and scissors, with a piece of bread for breakfast, in a bit of newspaper, carefully stuck two needles into the lapel of my coat and we started.

The shop was on Pelem Street, a shop district one block long and just wide enough for two ordinary sized wagons to pass each other. We stopped at a door where I noticed at once a brown shining porcelain knob and a half rubbed off number seven. Father looked at his watch and at me.

"Don't look so frightened," he said. "You need not go in until seven. Perhaps if you start in at this hour he will think you have been in the habit of beginning at seven and will not expect you to come in earlier. Remember, be independent. At seven o'clock rise and go home no matter whether the others go or stay." . . .

Now only I felt frightened, and waiting made me nervous, so I tried the knob. The door yielded heavily and closed slowly. I was half way up when it closed entirely, leaving me in darkness. I groped my way to the top of the stairs and hearing a clattering noise of machines, I felt about, found a door, and pushed it open and went in. A tall, dark, beardless man stood folding coats at a table. I went over and asked him for the name (I don't remember what it was). "Yes," he said crossly. "What do you want?"

I said, "I am the new feller hand." He looked at me from head to foot. My face felt so burning hot that I could scarcely see.

"It is more likely," he said, "that you can pull bastings than fell sleeve lining." Then turning from me he shouted over the noise of the machine: "Presser, is this the girl?" The presser put down the iron and looked at me. "I suppose so," he said, "I only know the father."

The cross man looked at me again and said, "Let's see what you can do." He kicked a chair, from which the back had been broken off, to the finisher's table, threw a coat upon it and said raising the corner of his mouth: "Make room for the new feller hand."

... I laid my coat down somewhere and pushed my bread into the sleeve. Then I stumbled into the bit of space made for me at the table, drew in the chair and sat down. The men were so close to me on each side I felt the heat of their bodies and could not prevent myself from shrinking away. The men noticed and probably felt hurt. One made a joke, the other laughed and the girls bent their heads low over their work. All at once the thought came: "If I don't do this coat quickly and well he will send me away at once." I picked up the coat, threaded my needle, and began hastily, repeating the lesson father impressed upon me. "Be careful not to twist the sleeve lining, take small false stitches."

My hands trembled so that I could not hold the needle properly. It took me a long while to do the coat. But at last it was done. I took it over to the boss and stood at the table waiting while he was examining it. He took long, trying every stitch with his needle. Finally he put it down and without looking at me gave me two other coats. I felt very happy! When I sat down at the table I drew my knees close together and stitched as quickly as I could.

When the pedlar came into the shop everybody bought rolls. I felt hungry but I was ashamed and would not eat the plain, heavy rye bread while the others ate rolls.

All day I took my finished work and laid it on the boss's table. He would glance at the clock and give me other work. Before the day was over I knew that this was a "piece work shop," that there were four machines and sixteen people were working. I also knew that I had done almost as much work as "the grown-up girls" and that they did not like me. I heard Betsy, the head feller hand, talking about "a snip of a girl coming and taking the very bread out of your mouth." The only one who could have been my friend was the presser who knew my father. But him I did not like. The worst I knew about him just now was that he was a soldier because the men called him so. But a soldier, I had learned, was capable of anything. And so, noticing that he looked at me often, I studiously kept my eyes from his corner of the room.

Seven o'clock came and every one worked on. I wanted to rise as father had told me to do and go home. But I had not the courage to stand up alone. I kept putting off going from minute to minute. My neck felt stiff and my back ached. I wished there were a back to my chair so that I could rest against it a little. When the people began to go home it seemed to me that it had been night a long time.

THE next morning when I came into the shop at seven o'clock, I saw at once that all the people were there and working as steadily as if they had been at work a long while. I had just time to put away my coat and go over to the table, when the boss shouted gruffly, "Look here, girl, if you want to work here you better come in early. No office hours in my shop." It seemed very still in the room, even the machines stopped. And his voice sounded dreadfully distinct. I hastened into the bit of space between the two men and sat down. He brought me two coats and snapped, "Hurry with these!"

From this hour a hard life began for me. He refused to employ me except by the week. He paid me three dollars and for this he hurried me from early until late. He gave me only two coats at a time to do. When I took them over and as he handed me the new work he would say quickly and sharply, "Hurry!" And when he did not say it in words he looked at me and I seemed to hear even more plainly, "Hurry!" I hurried but he was never satisfied. By looks and manner he made me feel that I was not doing enough. Late at night when the people would stand up and begin to fold their work away and I too would rise feeling stiff in every limb and thinking with dread of our cold empty little room and the uncooked rice, he would come over with still another coat.

"I need it the first thing in the morning," he would give as an excuse. I understood that he was taking advantage of me because I was a child. And now that it was dark in the shop except for the low single gas jet over my table and the one over his at the other end of the room, and there was no one to see, more tears fell on the sleeve lining as I bent over it than there were stitches in it.

I did not soon complain to father. I had given him an idea of the people and the work during the first days. But when I had been in the shop a few weeks I told him, "The boss is hurrying the life out of me." I know now that if I had put it less strongly he would have paid more attention to it. Father hated to hear things put strongly. Besides he himself worked very hard. He never came home before eleven and he left at five in the morning.

He said to me now, "Work a little longer until you have more experience; then you can be independent."

"But if I did piece work, father, I would not have to hurry so. And I could go home earlier when the other people go."

Father explained further, "It pays him better to employ you by the week. Don't you see if you did piece work he would have to pay you as much as he pays a woman piece worker? But this way he gets almost as much work out of you for half the amount a woman is paid."

I myself did not want to leave the shop for fear of losing a day or even more perhaps in finding other work. To lose half a dollar meant that it would take so much longer before mother and the children would come. And now I wanted them more than ever before. I longed for my mother and a home where it would be light and warm and she would be waiting when we came from work. Because I longed for them so I lived much in imagination. For so I could have them near me. Often as the hour for going home drew near I would sit stitching and making believe that mother and the children were home waiting. On leaving the shop I would hasten along through the street keeping my eyes on the ground so as to shut out everything but what I wanted to see. I pictured myself walking into the house. There was a delicious warm smell of cooked food. Mother greeted me near the door and the children gathered about me shouting and trying to pull me down. Mother scolded them saying, "Let her take her coat off, see how cold her hands are!" But they paid no attention and pulled me down to them. Their little arms were about my neck, their warm faces against my cold cheeks and we went tumbling all over each other. Soon mother called, "Supper is ready." There was a scampering and a rush to the table, followed by a scraping of chairs and a clattering of dishes. Finally we were all seated. There was browned meat and potatoes for supper.

I used to keep this up until I turned the key in the door and opened it and stood facing the dark, cold, silent room.

4

SADIE FROWNE

The Story of a Sweatshop Girl
September 25, 1902

Hamilton Holt, the publisher of the popular magazine The Independent, *attempted to educate his largely middle-class readership with a series of autobiographies of ordinary people with, as he put it, "undistinguished" lives. The story of Sadie Frowne, a young immigrant worker, appeared early in this series of "lifelets," which began in 1902 and ended in 1907. In this first-person account, Frowne describes the rhythms of labor and*

From Sadie Frowne, "The Story of a Sweatshop Girl," *The Independent* LIV (September 25, 1902): 2279–82.

leisure and emphasizes the important role of "put[ting] on plenty of style." Her essay corresponds to the rise of commercialized entertainment in urban America as wage-earning women like Frowne eagerly embraced the emerging culture of consumerism and leisure.

Miss Frowne is little more than sixteen years of age, and her story was consequently dictated to a representative of The Independent. *It was afterward read over to herself and relatives and pronounced accurate in all respects. Save for slight alterations of her language there is no deviation from the narrative. Brownsville is the Hebrew sweatshop quarter of Brooklyn, New York.*
                                                            —EDITOR [Hamilton Holt].

My mother was a tall, handsome, dark complexioned woman with red cheeks, large brown eyes and a great quantity of jet black, wavy hair. She was well educated, being able to talk in Russian, German, Polish and French, and even to read English print, tho, of course, she did not know what it meant. She kept a little grocer's shop in the little village where we lived at first. That was in Poland, somewhere on the frontier, and mother had charge of a gate between the countries, so that everybody who came through the gate had to show her a pass. She was much looked up to by the people, who used to come and ask her for advice. Her word was like law among them. . . .

When I was a little more than ten years of age my father died. He was a good man and a steady worker, and we never knew what it was to be hungry while he lived. After he died troubles began, for the rent of our shop was about $6 a month and then there were food and clothes to provide. We needed little, it is true, but even soup, black bread and onions we could not always get. . . .

Mother wrote to Aunt Fanny, who lived in New York, and told her how hard it was to live in Poland, and Aunt Fanny advised her to come and bring me. . . .

We came by steerage on a steamship in a very dark place that smelt dreadfully. There were hundreds of other people packed in with us, men, women and children, and almost all of them were sick. It took us twelve days to cross the sea, and we thought we should die, but at last the voyage was over, and we came up and saw the beautiful bay and the big woman with the spikes on her head and the lamp that is lighted at night in her hand (Goddess of Liberty).

Aunt Fanny and her husband met us at the gate of this country and were very good to us, and soon I had a place to live out (domestic servant), while my mother got work in a factory making white goods.

I was only a little over thirteen years of age and a greenhorn, so I received $9 a month and board and lodging, which I thought was doing well. Mother, who, as I have said, was very clever, made $9 a week on white goods, which means all sorts of underclothing, and is high class work.

But mother had a very gay disposition. She liked to go around and see everything, and friends took her about New York at night and she caught a bad cold and coughed and coughed. She really had hasty consumption, but she didn't know it, and I didn't know it, and she tried to keep on working, but it was no use. She had not the strength. Two doctors attended her, but they could do nothing, and at last she died and I was left alone. . . .

So I went to work in Allen street (Manhattan) in what they call a sweatshop, making skirts by machine. I was new at the work and the foreman scolded me a great deal.

"Now, then," he would say, "this place is not for you to be looking around in. Attend to your work. That is what you have to do."

I did not know at first that you must not look around and talk, and I made many mistakes with the sewing, so that I was often called a "stupid animal." But I made $4 a week by working six days in the week. For there are two Sabbaths here—our own Sabbath, that comes on a Saturday, and the Christian Sabbath that comes on Sunday. It is against our law to work on our own Sabbath, so we work on their Sabbath. . . .

I lived at this time with a girl named Ella, who worked in the same factory and made $5 a week. We had the room all to ourselves, paying $1.50 a week for it, and doing light housekeeping. It was in Allen street, and the window looked out of the back, which was good, because there was an elevated railroad in front, and in summer time a great deal of dust and dirt came in at the front windows. We were on the fourth story and could see all that was going on in the back rooms of the houses behind us, and early in the morning the sun used to come in our window. . . .

It cost me $2 a week to live, and I had a dollar a week to spend on clothing and pleasure, and saved the other dollar. I went to night school, but it was hard work learning at first as I did not know much English.

Two years ago I came to this place, Brownsville, where so many of my people are, and where I have friends. I got work in a factory making underskirts—all sorts of cheap underskirts, like cotton and calico for the summer and woolen for the winter, but never the silk, satin or velvet underskirts. I earned $4.50 a week and lived on $2 a week, the same as before.

I got a room in the house of some friends who lived near the factory. I pay $1 a week for the room and am allowed to do light housekeeping—that is, cook my meals in it. . . . My food for a week costs a dollar, just as it did in Allen street, and I have the rest of my money to do as I like with. I am earning $5.50 a week now, and will probably get another increase soon.

. . . The factory is in the third story of a brick building. It is in a room twenty feet long and fourteen broad. There are fourteen machines in it. I and the daughter of the people with whom I live work two of these machines. The other operators are all men, some young and some old.

At first a few of the young men were rude. When they passed me they would touch my hair and talk about my eyes and my red cheeks, and make jokes. I cried and said that if they did not stop I would leave the place. The boss said that that should not be, that no one must annoy me. Some of the other men stood up for me, too, especially Henry, who said two or three times that he wanted to fight. Now the men all treat me very nicely. It was just that some of them did not know better, not being educated.

Henry is tall and dark, and he has a small mustache. His eyes are brown and large. He is pale and much educated, having been to school. He knows a great many things and has some money saved. I think nearly $400. He is not going to be in a sweatshop all the time, but will soon be in the real estate business, for a lawyer that knows him well has promised to open an office and pay him to manage it.

Henry has seen me home every night for a long time and makes love to me.[1] He wants me to marry him, but I am not seventeen yet, and I think that is too young. He is only nineteen, so we can wait.

I have been to the fortune teller's three or four times, and she always tells me that tho I have had such a lot of trouble I am to be very rich and happy. I believe her because she has told so many things that have come true. So I will keep on working in the factory for a time. Of course it is hard, but I would have to work hard even if I was married.

---

[1] *makes love to*: romances.

I get up at half-past five o'clock every morning and make myself a cup of coffee on the oil stove. I eat a bit of bread and perhaps some fruit and then go to work. Often I get there soon after six o'clock so as to be in good time, tho the factory does not open till seven. I have heard that there is a sort of clock that calls you at the very time you want to get up, but I can't believe that because I don't see how the clock would know.

At seven o'clock we all sit down to our machines and the boss brings to each one the pile of work that he or she is to finish during the day, what they call in English their "stint." This pile is put down beside the machine and as soon as a skirt is done it is laid on the other side of the machine. Sometimes the work is not all finished by six o'clock and then the one who is behind must work overtime. Sometimes one is finished ahead of time and gets away at four or five o'clock, but generally we are not done till six o'clock.

The machines go like mad all day, because the faster you work the more money you get. Sometimes in my haste I get my finger caught and the needle goes right through it. It goes so quick, tho, that it does not hurt much. I bind the finger up with a piece of cotton and go on working. We all have accidents like that. Where the needle goes through the nail it makes a sore finger, or where it splinters a bone it does much harm. Sometimes a finger has to come off. Generally, tho, one can be cured by a salve.

All the time we are working the boss walks about examining the finished garments and making us do them over again if they are not just right. So we have to be careful as well as swift. But I am getting so good at the work that within a year I will be making $7 a week, and then I can save at least $3.50 a week. I have over $200 saved now.

The machines are all run by foot power, and at the end of the day one feels so weak that there is a great temptation to lie right down and sleep. But you must go out and get air, and have some pleasure. So instead of lying down I go out, generally with Henry. Sometimes we go to Coney Island, where there are good dancing places, and sometimes we go to Ulmer Park to picnics. I am very fond of dancing, and, in fact, all sorts of pleasure. I go to the theater quite often, and like those plays that make you cry a great deal. "The Two Orphans" is good. Last time I saw it I cried all night because of the hard times that the children had in the play. I am going to see it again when it comes here.

For the last two winters I have been going to night school at Public School 84 on Glenmore avenue. I have learned reading, writing and arithmetic. I can read quite well in English now and I look at the newspapers every day. I read English books, too, sometimes. The last one that I read was "A Mad Marriage," by Charlotte Braeme. She's a grand writer and makes things just like real to you. You feel as if you were the poor girl yourself going to get married to a rich duke.

I am going back to night school again this winter. Plenty of my friends go there. Some of the women in my class are more than forty years of age. Like me, they did not have a chance to learn anything in the old country. It is good to have an education; it makes you feel higher. Ignorant people are all low. People say now that I am clever and fine in conversation.

We have just finished a strike in our business. It spread all over and the United Brotherhood of Garment Workers was in it. That takes in the cloakmakers, coatmakers, and all the others. We struck for shorter hours, and after being out four weeks won the fight. We only have to work nine and a half hours a day and we get the same pay as before. So the union does good after all in spite of what some people say against it—that it just takes our money and does nothing.

I pay 25 cents a month to the union, but I do not begrudge that because it is for our benefit. The next strike is going to be for a raise of wages, which we all ought to have. But tho I belong to the Union I am not a Socialist or an Anarchist. I don't know exactly what those things mean. . . .

Some of the women blame me very much because I spend so much money on clothes. They say that instead of a dollar a week I ought not to spend more than twenty-five cents a week on clothes, and that I should save the rest. But a girl must have clothes if she is to go into high society at Ulmer Park or Coney Island or the theatre. Those who blame me are the old country people who have old-fashioned notions, but the people who have been here a long time know better. A girl who does not dress well is stuck in a corner, even if she is pretty, and Aunt Fanny says that I do just right to put on plenty of style.

I have many friends and we often have jolly parties. Many of the young men like to talk to me, but I don't go out with any except Henry.

5

CLARA LEMLICH

Life in the Shop

November 26, 1909

A Russian Jewish immigrant, Clara Lemlich arrived in the Lower East Side at age sixteen and immediately began working to support her family. After work, she walked to the New York Public Library, where she read the Russian classics and attended evening classes to learn English. Although exposed to revolutionary literature in Russia, Lemlich recalled that she "knew very little about Socialism." Angered by the conditions of work she confronted daily in America—working seventy hours but never earning "enough to keep body and soul together"—she embraced socialism and trade unionism, helping form Local 25 of the ILGWU in 1905. Described as a "pint size of trouble for the bosses," Lemlich delivered a passionate call for a general strike, and within two days 20,000 shirtwaist makers had walked off their jobs.

First let me tell you something about the way we work and what we are paid. There are two kinds of work—regular, that is salary work, and piece work. The regular work pays about $6 a week and the girls have to be at their machines at 7 o'clock in the morning and they stay at them until 8 o'clock at night, with just one-half hour for lunch in that time.

The work is all divided up. No girl ever makes a whole waist. There are examiners and finishers. They all get different pay for their work, but it runs only from $3 or $4 a week[;] the finishers make to the $6 or sometimes $7 a week the cutters and some others make.

The shops. Well, there is just one row of machines that the daylight ever gets to—that is the front row, nearest the window. The girls at all the other rows of machines back in the shops have to work by gaslight, by day as well as by night. Oh, yes, the shops keep the work going at night, too.

From *New York Evening Journal*, November 26, 1909, p. 3. Lemlich's quotations are from Annelise Orleck, *Common Sense and a Little Fire: Women and Working-Class Politics in the United States, 1900–1965* (Chapel Hill: University of North Carolina Press, 1995), 33–34.

The bosses in the shops are hardly what you would call educated men. And the girls to them are part of the machines they are running. They yell at the girls and they "call them down" even worse than I imagine the negro slaves were in the South. They don't use very nice language. They swear at us and sometimes do worse—they call us names that are not pretty to hear.

There are no dressing rooms for the girls in the shops. They have to hang up their hats and coats—such as they are—on hooks along the walls. Sometimes a girl has a new hat. It never is much to look at because it never costs more than fifty cents, but it's pretty sure to be spoiled after it's been at the shop.

We're human, all of us girls, and we're young. We like new hats as well as any other young women. Why shouldn't we? And if one of us gets a new one, even if it hasn't cost more than fifty cents, that means that we have gone for weeks on two-cent lunches—dry cake and nothing else.

I have known many girls who were never able to buy a hat at all. Lots of them don't wear any, Winter or Summer. They are the ones who earn $3 a week. They take the clothes of the girls better off— those who earn $6 or $7 a week—after they have really been worn out. That's how they manage to get along. They never buy any clothes of their own.

Seventy-five cents is the most a girl can pay for a pair of shoes. And she has to wear them a long time—and she does. Some girls can buy only one, perhaps two shirtwaists a year—while they help to make thousands of them. They make their own dresses after they have worked thirteen or fourteen hours a day, made with remnants that cost altogether $1 or $1.50.

The shops are unsanitary—that's the word that is generally used, but there ought to be a worse one used. Whenever we tear or damage any of the goods we sew on, or whenever it is found damaged after we are through with it, whether we have done it or not, we are charged for the piece and sometimes for a whole yard of the material—perhaps $1 or $1.50.

At the beginning of every slow season, $2 is deducted from our salaries. We have never been able to find out what this is for.

2

Triangle and the
"Uprising of Twenty Thousand"

6

THE NEW YORK TIMES

Arrest Strikers for Being Assaulted
November 5, 1909

This report from the New York Times *tells of the arrest of Mary Dreier, president of New York's WTUL, while she picketed the Triangle Waist Company even before the general strike in late November 1909. Mary Dreier and her sister Margaret inherited in 1897 the family fortune upon the death of their father, a wealthy German American business leader who made his fortune in the iron industry. They both joined the WTUL in 1904 and, despite their lack of experience in labor organization, became ardent advocates for women workers and trade unionism.*

Policeman Joseph De Cantillon of the Mercer Street Station—the "Penitentiary Precinct" of the Police Department—arrested yesterday morning Miss Mary Dreier, President of the Women's Trade Union League, a wealthy champion of laboring women in this city, because she advised a young woman operative, hurrying to the lofts of the Triangle Waist Company of 29 Washington Place, that there was a strike there, and urged her not to be a strikebreaker.

This, however, Miss Dreier said last night was only the latest of a series of outrages which had been perpetrated by men of the "peniten-

From "Arrest Strikers for Being Assaulted," *New York Times*, November 5, 1909, p. 1.

tiary precinct" for months. Miss Dreier asserted that upon every occasion the police have taken the part of the shop owners in Washington Place and the surrounding neighborhood where there have been strikes of women operatives in the last few months. The police, said Miss Dreier, always arrest the pickets put out by the striking girls, even when the pickets have been beaten, in the presence of the police, by strikebreakers, both men and women.

In the case of her own arrest yesterday morning Miss Dreier said that the young woman whom she had accosted, Miss Anna Walla of 437 East Twelfth Street, had struck her with her fist, yet De Cantillon, on Miss Walla's complaint that Miss Dreier had annoyed her, seized Miss Dreier.

At the station Lieut. Von Derzelsky told her that her arrest had been a mistake and that she was at liberty to go. She did not remain to make a complaint against De Cantillon nor against Miss Walla, although at her home, 144 East Sixty-fifth Street, she said last night that she had protested to De Cantillon, when he arrested her, that Miss Walla had delivered the blow, and not she.

Just why the police have so openly sided with the employers, as Miss Dreier charged, she declared she did not know, but among the employes in many of the shops the reason was boldly stated to be that the employers had "sugared" the police. This charge is being made upon every side.

Women Unionist's Story

Miss Dreier, who is a frail young woman and speaks with a foreign accent, said that about 150 girls were on strike. The Woman's Trades Union League, of which she is the President, is backing them in their fight against Harris & Blanck, owners of the Triangle Waist Company. The strike, she said, began about five weeks ago. The girls were "locked out," the owners of the factory giving as a reason that they had no work for them to do.

"When these girls were discharged," said Miss Dreier, "they took the excuse 'no more work at present' in good faith, and left without a murmur, although they are all poor girls, most of them foreigners, who find it hard to make both ends meet. Imagine their surprise when a day or two following their discharge they read advertisements in the papers for girls to take their places in the factory. Then the lockout became a strike.

"The Woman's Trades Union League became interested in the matter, and a committee in charge of Miss Violet Pike was named to take charge of the picketing. Policemen were sent to the place, some of them in plain clothes, and from the first they have all apparently been in sympathy with the employers. They have arrested many of the girls, and have been telling us we were doing wrong when we talked to the strikebreaking girls about what they were doing, despite the fact that, as we all know, moral suasion in such matters is legal.

Was Keeping within the Law

"Whenever we spoke to the girls the police would come up and gruffly order us to stop talking, and when we asserted our legal rights in the matter, persisted in their refusal to allow us to talk. As to the incident this morning, which resulted in my arrest, I am glad of the chance to tell the facts.

"I was crossing the street to see a girl who was on the way to the factory. One of the plain clothes men stopped me with the excuse as that I was obstructing a public highway. I insisted on my rights, and told him I would continue to act as I had been acting, as I knew the law and was careful to keep within it.

"The only thing I said to the girl was 'There's a strike in the Triangle.' She became very angry and talked about my annoying her. Then she struck me. When she struck me I turned to the policeman to see if he would arrest her, as he had been doing in the case of the striking girls. The girl told him that I had been annoying and threatening her, whereupon the policeman turned to her and said, 'If you want to press the charge, come along to the station house with me.'

Released at the Station

"In the station the girl told the Lieutenant behind the desk that I said, 'I will split your head open if you try to go to work.' That was so palpably false that the Lieutenant refused to listen further and released me. Of course, I shall continue my work on behalf of the girls." . . .

Thugs Hired for Intimidation

The charge is made that thugs have been hired to intimidate the pickets. This has been heard in the precinct for months. At the time of the neckwear strike, ended a few weeks ago, it was asserted that bands of "strong-arm men" were imported from the Bowery and the regions east of it by certain employers to intimidate the strikers. The intimidation took the form of beatings. It is a fact that one young girl was confined to her bed for three weeks as the result of the treatment at the hands of half a dozen of these thugs.

Miss Elsie Cole, a graduate of Vassar and a member of the Woman's Trade Union League, has been helping the Triangle girl strikers. She told [of] some of her experiences with the police yesterday. They were similar to those of Miss Dreier. She declared that one policeman, when she quoted to him the law permitting her to use moral suasion in influencing strikebreakers so long as she did not try and influence them by acts expressing or implying threats, intimidations, coercion, or force, exclaimed:

"Well, you know me, young lady. None of that around here."

Miss Marot[1] declares that when she was on picket duty a plain-clothes man said to her: "You out-of-town scum, keep out of this or you'll find yourself in jail."

When this remark was reported to Inspector Daly at the hearing the committee says he replied:

"Well, scum might be a nice word. How do I know what it means?"

[1] *Miss Marot*: Helen Marot, secretary of the Trade Union League.

7

ALLAN L. BENSON

Women in a Labor War: How the Working Girls of New York East Side Have Learned to Use Men's Weapons in a Struggle for Better Conditions

April 1910

A Socialist and author of numerous books and pamphlets, Allan Benson wrote frequently on trade unionism and labor strikes. His Socialist beliefs caused him to be surprised by what he regarded as extraordinary support for the women strikers from women of means, adding that they had become "sisters under the skin." Benson's essay was published in Munsey's Magazine,

From Allan L. Benson, "Women in a Labor War: How the Working Girls of New York East Side Have Learned to Use Men's Weapons in a Struggle for Better Conditions," *Munsey's Magazine* XLIII (April 1910): 68–76.

an inexpensive journal created by Frank Munsey to provide a "magazine of the people and for the people, with pictures and art and good cheer and human interest throughout."

Women who do men's work are fighting their battles with men's weapons—fighting more courageously than most men do.

Three thousand girls had assembled in the Cooper Union, New York—the building in which Abraham Lincoln made his famous oration in the year before the outbreak of the Civil War. The girls were shirtwaist-makers. They had gathered to decide whether the thirty thousand young women engaged in the same work in New York should institute a general strike.

A number of speeches were made. There were many "ifs," "maybes," and "buts." All of the speakers seemed to have their minds on the thermometer—for it was cold outside.

Suddenly, a slip of a girl rose in the body of the hall. She asked to be permitted to speak. The chairman didn't know her. She was interrupting the program. He wanted to introduce somebody else: but a ripple of cheers caused him to give the girl the permission she sought.

She threaded her way through the crowded aisles to the platform. The spectators saw that, in years, she was little more than a child. That didn't matter. Most of the shirtwaist girls were little more than children. Few were above twenty: many were sixteen, and even fourteen. So they were glad to listen to another who was little more than a child.

She began in a plaintive tone, speaking simply in her native Yiddish: but her simple words seemed barbed with fire. Outsiders who could not understand Yiddish were unable to comprehend what was happening. The great audience, which had been almost indifferent to the other speakers, suddenly became demonstrative. Every girl was on her feet—cheering more and more enthusiastically.

This is what the little shirtwaist girl said, in effect:

"I am a working girl—one of those who are suffering from intolerable conditions. I thought we came here to decide whether we should all go on a strike. The speakers seem to think that we came here only to talk. I am tired of so much talk. We have only one thing to do—to vote to strike or not to strike. For my part, I offer a resolution that we go on a strike—*now.*"

Then the little girl disappeared through the wings to return to her seat. She never reached her seat. There was too much confusion—too much cheering; there were too many outstretched hands. And one of those hands pulled her into a seat far down in front.

When the tumult subsided, the chairman bethought himself of his parliamentary law. No resolution could be put to a vote without a seconder—and the little girl's resolution to strike *now* had not been seconded. Did anybody care to second it?

Did anybody care to second it? Why, there wasn't a girl in the hall, apparently, who would not have fought her way over the footlights, if necessary, to second it. Everybody seconded it; and a moment later, when the resolution was put to a vote, everybody voted for it.

The strike was on! One small voice had called out thirty thousand girls; called them out at the beginning of winter; called them out when their immediate and imperative needs were calling them back. . . .

A Typical Immigrant's Story

In order to understand all this, it is well to know the story of Clara Lemlich, the girl who spoke in Yiddish. Clara Lemlich was born in Russia, of Jewish parents. Her mother was a peasant; her grandmother was a peasant; her great-grandmother, all her feminine ancestors, so far as she knew, were peasants. . . .

The cruelty of the Russian government toward the Jews caused her parents to flee from the country; and they came to America, bringing with them their little girl.

The family settled in New York. Driven by the blows of poverty, they were wedged into that great East Side which, always bulging, still seems never too full to hold another. The father could not earn enough to support the family. Rent was too high, food too high, clothing too high, wages too low. The mother must help. She was used to helping. . . .

The East Side quickly told her what she could do. The women of the East Side had felt the spur that was forcing women to do men's work. The East Side told Clara Lemlich's mother that she should take her place in a factory. It told her she should sit before a sewing-machine run by a dynamo, and sew all day. She could make more shirtwaists than she could wear out in a thousand lifetimes, but she could have none of them unless she bought them. She could have only wages. Other women would wear the shirtwaists. . . .

Clara Organizes a Union

As soon as Clara was old enough to guide a piece of cloth under a needle, she also heard the call to the factory, and like her mother, answered it without a murmur. But the air of America, breathed in her childhood when her views of life were still forming, had done something for her that it had not done for her mother. It had made her think. It had made her aspire to better things. It had made her want things that her employer was unwilling to give.

Somewhere, she heard that labor unions could make employers give more things. She inquired about labor unions. It all seemed so simple, when she heard it. Everybody should just get together and say:

"Give us such and such things, or we'll stop work!"

In the mind of this poor peasant girl, the news produced the hot zeal that ever characterizes a new convert to any cause. She would urge all the girls who made shirtwaists to join the union. She would convert the girls in the factory in which she worked, and then go to the five hundred other factories, in which forty thousand other girls worked. She would—oh, but there was hardly a limit to what she would do. She would make all the girls happy, including herself. . . .

So it was with Clara Lemlich's confidence in her ability to organize into a labor union the girls employed in the New York shirtwaist industry. She approached her task eagerly—almost feverishly. To girl after girl she told in turn how much there was to win—how easily it could be won. Just organize: join the union—that was all. No more scanty breakfasts, cold rooms, or clothing too thin to keep the body warm! Every worker would get plenty of the necessaries and even of the comforts of life. . . .

Of a hundred girls whom Clara Lemlich canvassed, she found only five who were willing to join the union. She organized the five. She got a charter, and started a branch union, with herself as the sixth member. She rented a little room in the heart of the East Side, where, for the payment of fifty cents a week, they were permitted to meet every seventh day. . . .

The Beginning of the Strike

. . . Clara Lemlich led out the girls in her factory, almost a month before the other thirty thousand came out. . . .

When Lincoln, a year or so after his great speech in the Cooper Union, called for volunteers, he experienced one sensation that later came to Clara Lemlich. Lincoln was swamped with offers to join the army. After Clara led her fellow workers out of the factory, she was swamped with offers to join the union.

Mind you, Clara was not the whole union. Her little body was only a branch of the main body, which had five hundred members; but, as soon as Clara and her shopmates struck, there was a rush from all of the other factories to become organized. . . . Everybody felt that there was to be trouble, and every girl sought the shelter of the union. Applications came so rapidly that, in some instances, it was impossible even to record them properly. . . .

Women Using Men's Weapons

. . . [Women] found themselves in a tight corner—pressed by hunger, pressed by cold, pressed by unfulfilled desires of many sorts. Concerted action promised the only hope of success. None could win unless all would stand together; and these Jewish girls fitted the old weapon to the new emergency. They invoked the subtle power of the ancient oath of their race. . . .

Some of the richest women in the country felt it. Mrs. O. H. P. Belmont, mother of the Duchess of Marlborough, felt it. Miss Anne Morgan, daughter of J. Pierpont Morgan, felt it. . . .

But the spur did more. It caused the women whom it had driven into factories to act like men who work in factories. Men who thus work do not weep or mourn when things in the factories pass beyond what they conceive to be their endurance. They strike. Not only do they strike, but they stick to their colors and battle for their cause as long as they have strength to do so. Yet no man ever gave a greater exhibition of dogged determination to persevere to the end than did these girls not yet out of their teens.

A Typical Labor War

When they "picketed" the factories and tried to prevent other women from taking their places, there were excitement and some disorder in the streets. In the scuffling, some of the girls were grabbed by the hair, and their heads were bumped against the curbstones. Never mind—let the strike go on! . . .

Yes, indeed, women have changed.

Fifty years ago, women would never have waged such a desperate fight, in mid-winter, against five hundred employers. They hadn't been prepared. They hadn't learned to fight the world as men fight it for a living. But they are learning—learning in the same school in which man learned.

8

THE NEW YORK TIMES

Church to the Aid of Girl Strikers

December 20, 1909

Rose Schneiderman, recognized for her spirited defense of unionism, emerged as a significant leader and fundraiser during the general strike. A Polish Jewish immigrant, Schneiderman went to work at age thirteen and later joined the WTUL and the Socialist party. In 1906 she was elected vice president of New York's WTUL and, despite their class differences, enjoyed a close and long friendship with its president, Mary Dreier.

Although women union leaders, including Schneiderman, remained ambivalent about support from the "mink brigade," few wealthy women rivaled Alva Belmont in her commitment to the strikers and to all working women. Few women also alienated the judges so completely that they bristled at her appearance in night court to bail out strikers. In turn, Belmont publicly rebuked them by name and fiercely repudiated the police for arresting the strikers. Magistrates complained that the generosity of women like Belmont emboldened picketers and prolonged the strike. To counter her efforts, they issued larger fines, set higher bonds, or sent women directly to jail.

Miss Rose Schneiderman, the little woman who is leading the striking shirtwaist makers in their fight for a recognition of their union and a fifty-two-hour working week, occupied the pulpit of the Manhattan Congregationalist Church last night. She was there at the request of the Rev. Dr. Henry A. Stimson, pastor of the church.

When she concluded her plea in behalf of the 7,000 girls who are still out, Dr. Stimson asked that everybody present join in a collection, the proceeds of which were to be given to Miss Schneiderman as a Christmas present for the girls, whose Christmas, he said, must of necessity be a sorry one. . . .

From "Church to the Aid of Girl Strikers," *New York Times*, December 20, 1909, pp. 1–2.

She Answered All Questions

... One of the women in the congregation suggested a way of helping the girls that brought tears to Miss Schneiderman's eyes. This woman asked if the girls could not be employed in the homes of private families, for the purpose of making shirtwaists, and she wanted to know if a request for such work would be attended to by the leaders. Miss Schneidermann replied that many of the girls were skilled at needlework and that many would be glad to get such work pending the settling of the strike.

"About three months ago," Miss Schneiderman said in her talk from the pulpit, "a group of about three hundred girls were locked out. Why? Because they joined a trades union. It was not a question of higher wages, but one of organization. ...

"Since the Cooper Union mass meeting hundreds of our girls have been arrested and some of them, poor and hard-pressed as they are, have been fined $5 and in a number of cases $10 each. Only a few days ago twelve of the girls were sent to the workhouse for five days, and as yet we have been unable to find out what the excuse was for sending them to that place. This struggle means, it seems, that though women are the wards of the State our guardians are taking very little care of us.

"My friends, the men are organized and they have gained an eight-hour day, which has made them stronger and better citizens, and their pay as a result of organization has been increased and they live better lives and have time to read and become improved morally as well as physically.

"The women having seen these things, also want the benefits of organization. We have found that individually we don't amount to much, for it is easy for them to replace us, and then you must remember that although a woman is working to-day she may and probably will be a mother of the future.

"The girls believe that they are entitled to have better pay and to have better food. In their case it is the same as in every other walk of life, for the world is full of good things and happiness and goodness, and why should not these girls have the part of it to which they are entitled?

"At this moment there are still 7,000 girls who are on strike, and the manufacturers who oppose their organizing have themselves organized to fight them. I ask you to take up this matter and look into it; take up the matter of those twelve girls who are in the Workhouse; take up the cruelties of the police, who not only arrest them, but also sometimes treat them shamefully.

"You read editorials about cruelty to birds because women wear bird feathers on their hats. Do you ever stop to think that nearly everything else you wear is the product of some poor girl's hard work, who at least should be entitled to equal consideration with the birds?" . . .

Mrs. Belmont on Girls' Bond

GIVES HER TOWN HOUSE AS BAIL FOR FOUR
STRIKERS—ALL NIGHT IN COURT

A heart-warming triumph awaits five girl pickets who come back this morning from Blackwell's Island, where they have been for five days. They were arrested doing picket duty in front of the shirtwaist factories out of which the strikers are trying to keep non-union girls.

The boat that brings them back from the Island will be met at the foot of East Twenty-sixth Street at 9 o'clock by hundreds of their sister strikers, who will cheer them for suffering in the cause for which they are all fighting. Miss Mary E. Dreier of the Woman's Trades Union League will have charge of the demonstration.

Mrs. O. H. P. Belmont had to remain in the Night Court yesterday morning until its close so that she might offer bail for four girls who had been arrested on Saturday night. The prisoners for whom she waited were Florence Milligan, 308 Stanton Street; Fannie Freedman, 308 Stanton Street; Sarah Sirnbaum, 1,504 Prospect Avenue, Brooklyn, and Alice Heimsblot, 129 East 109th Street.

Magistrate Butts held the girls in $100 bail for examination to-night, and remarked that he would require $800 surety for the four. Mrs. Belmont's lawyer, who had been in court all night, had with him deeds that he was to use as bail bonds. But when the four girls came to trial the lawyer could not be found.

"Very well," said Mrs. Belmont, "if he is not here I can give my home at 477 Madison Avenue as bond for these girls to appear on Monday night."

Not recognizing the volunteer bailer, Magistrate Butts asked her if she was sure the house was worth $800.

"I think it is," replied Mrs. Belmont. "It is valued at $400,000. There may be a mortgage on it for $100,000."

The girls were then freed on this bail.

9

WILLIAM MAILLY

The Working Girls' Strike

December 23, 1909

*William Mailly worked briefly as a coal miner and served as the na-
tional secretary of the Socialist party before becoming editor of several
labor newspapers. Sympathetic to the strikers, Mailly penned a number
of essays about the "great uprising." He subsequently wrote about the fire
and the relief effort for survivors and victims' families for the American
Federation of Labor's newspaper, the* American Federationist.

What do the strikers want? Narrowed down, the main issue is recognition of the union. On that hinge all the other questions at issue, for the
union officials declare no other questions can be settled unless that
one is settled. The employers' association as emphatically declares
against the union and for the "open shop."

Conditions in the shirtwaist making trade are bad. The wages generally are low, the hours worked per day are many, the shops, especially the smaller ones, poorly ventilated, dark and unsanitary. . . .

In the busy season work is rushed night and day and frequently on
Sundays. Then comes the long period of semi-idleness when the workers have to wait until the busy season begins again and many of them
are out of work altogether. . . .

What has been gained? In the first place, the strike came at the
highest point of the busy season. It caught the manufacturers totally
unprepared, with large orders on their hands, every available machine
going and every available employee at work. It could not have come at
a more opportune time for the workers. As a result, from the first
hour there was a rush of employers to union headquarters to sign the
union agreement. To date 236 shops have signed up, involving nearly
17,000 people. This means not only the establishment of the union in
these shops but also a radical increase in wages in many of them.

From William Mailly, "The Working Girls' Strike," *The Independent* LXVII (December
23, 1909): 1416–20.

Ninety-six shops, at this writing, are still to settle. In the meanwhile, the non-union employers are running short on filling orders, the busy season is at its height, and the union employers are getting further into the market. . . .

To sum up, three things are notable about this strike: In every shop there are always a few girls in the lead. Some of these have been agitating for a long time, some are new and are having their first experience as leaders. But these leaders are invariably the best paid, the ones who get the most wages, in each shop. They are the ones who have less reason to complain. They have carried their sisters along with them by very force of their own determination and the spirit of resistance to the general conditions prevailing. One has but to associate with these fine, high-strung, intelligent and courageous girls to appreciate their moral caliber and their capacity for self-sacrifice and devotion.

Secondly, while the majority of the shirtwaist makers are Jews, and the union business is usually conducted in Jewish, yet they have succeeded in getting 3,000 Italians to strike with them. It has been difficult to reach the Italians heretofore and get them into the union. Now the start has been made and a separate Italian headquarters established, with special Italian literature and Italian speakers; it is believed the workers of this nationality are permanently enlisted in the union cause.

Lastly, the comparatively minor role played by men, both in numbers and in direction, is something new in the history of labor strikes in this country. The principal union officials are men, it is true, but the strike has been inspired by women; it is mainly women who have done the picketing, been arrested, fined, run the risk of assault, received ill-treatment from police and police courts alike, and shown themselves eager to sacrifice without stint to bring about better conditions in the shops and factories.

Such a spectacle, covering such a wide area, involving so many interests, social and personal, moral and material, embracing so much of moment to the community, is without parallel. Coming at a time when the movement of women for greater political and economic recognition is commanding the attention of the civilized world, this remarkable strike of girls in New York is symbolic of how deeply-rooted among women that movement has become and the vast sweep and influence it is destined hereafter to assume in the industrial and political life of this nation.

10

The Uprising of the Twenty Thousands
(Dedicated to the Waistmakers of 1909)
1910

The general strike transformed the ILGWU, breathing new life into the organization and swelling its membership almost overnight. The 1909 strike of women also helped pave the way for a successful strike in 1910 by the predominantly male cloakmakers. The uprising assumed a central role in the educational program of the union and in its overall history, and this song remained popular years after the strike.

In the black of the winter of nineteen nine,
When we froze and bled on the picket line,
We showed the world that women could fight
And we rose and won with women's might.

Chorus:
Hail the waistmakers of nineteen nine,
Making their stand on the picket line,
Breaking the power of those who reign,
Pointing the way, smashing the chain.

And we gave new courage to the men
Who carried on in nineteen ten
And shoulder to shoulder we'll win through,
Led by the I.L.G.W.U.

Let's Sing! Educational Department, ILGWU, from the Triangle Web Site of the Kheel Center, Cornell University. http://www.ilr.cornell.edu/trianglefire/texts/songs/uprising .html. Accessed on December 15, 2006.

3

The Triangle Tragedy: Grief and Outrage

11

THE NEW YORK WORLD

The Triangle Fire

March 27, 1911

William Shepherd was on assignment for the United Press agency when he happened upon the Triangle fire. An accomplished reporter, he immediately telephoned the story to his boss, detailing the tragedy as he watched from across the street. His account was transmitted and reprinted in newspapers throughout the country.

At 4:35 o'clock Saturday afternoon, fire springing from a source that may never be positively identified was discovered in the rear of the eighth floor of the ten-story building at the northwest corner of Washington Place and Greene Street, the first of three floors occupied as a factory by the Triangle Waist Company. . . .

More than a third of those who lost their lives did so in jumping from windows. The firemen who answered the first of the four alarms turned in found thirty bodies on the pavements of Washington Place and Greene Street. . . .

Every available ambulance in Manhattan was called upon to cart the dead to the morgue—bodies charred to unrecognizable blackness or reddened to a sickly hue—as was to be seen by shoulders or limbs

From William Shepherd, "The Triangle Fire," *New York World*, March 27, 1911 (Thrice-A-Week Edition), p. 1.

protruding through flame-eaten clothing. Men and women, boys and girls were of the dead that littered the street; that is actually the condition—the streets were littered.

The fire began in the eighth story. The flames licked and shot their way up through the other two stories. All three floors were occupied by the Triangle Waist Company. The estimate of the number of employees at work is made by Chief Croker at about 1,000. The proprietors of the company say 700 men and girls were in their place.

Whatever the number, they had no chance of escape. Before smoke or flame gave signs from the windows, the loss of life was fully under way. The first signs that persons in the street knew that these three top stories had turned into red furnaces in which human creatures were being caught and incinerated was when screaming men and women and boys and girls crowded out on the many window ledges and threw themselves into the streets far below.

They jumped with their clothing ablaze. The hair of some of the girls streamed up aflame as they leaped. Thud after thud sounded on the pavements. It is a ghastly fact that on both the Greene Street and Washington Place sides of the building there grew mounds of the dead and dying.

And the worst horror of all was that in this heap of the dead now and then there stirred a limb or sounded a moan.

Within the three flaming floors it was as frightful. There flames enveloped many so that they died instantly. When Fire Chief Croker could make his way into these three floors, he found sights that utterly staggered him, that sent him, a man used to viewing horrors, back and down into the street with quivering lips.

The floors were black with smoke. And then he saw as the smoke drifted away bodies burned to bare bones. There were skeletons bending over sewing machines.

The elevator boys saved hundreds. They each made twenty trips from the time of the alarm until twenty minutes later when they could do no more. Fire was streaming into the shaft, flames biting at the cables. They fled for their own lives.

Some, about seventy, chose a successful avenue of escape. They clambered up a ladder to the roof. A few remembered the fire escape. Many may have thought of it but only as they uttered cries of dismay.

Wretchedly inadequate was this fire escape—a lone ladder running down to a rear narrow court, which was smoke filled as the fire raged, one narrow door giving access to the ladder. By the score they fought and struggled and breathed fire and died trying to make that needle-eye road to self-preservation.

Those who got [to] the roof—got life. . . . [But] those who did make the fire escape . . . huddled themselves into what appeared as bad a trap as the one from which they had escaped. . . .

Shivering at the chasm below them, scorched by the fire behind, there were some that still held positions on the window sills when the first squad of firemen arrived. The nets were spread below with all promptness. Citizens were commandeered into service, as the firemen necessarily gave their attention to the one engine and hose of the force that first arrived.

The catapult force that the bodies gathered in the long plunges made the nets utterly without avail. Screaming girls and men, as they fell, tore the nets from the grasp of the holders, and the bodies struck the sidewalks and lay just as they fell. Some of the bodies ripped big holes through the life nets. . . .

Concentrated, the fire burned within. The flames caught all the flimsy lace stuff and linens that go into the making of spring and summer shirtwaists and fed eagerly upon the rolls of silk.

The cutting room was laden with the stuff on long tables. The employees were toiling over such material at the rows and rows of machines. Sinisterly the spring day gave aid to the fire. Many of the window panes facing south and east were drawn down. Draughts had full play.

The experts say that the three floors must each have become a whirlpool of fire. Whichever way the entrapped creatures fled they met a curving sweep of flame. Many swooned and died. Others fought their way to the windows or the elevator or fell fighting for a chance at the fire escape, the single fire escape leading into the blind court that was to be reached from the upper floors by clambering over a window sill!

On all of the three floors, at a narrow window, a crowd met death trying to get out to that one slender fire escape ladder.

It was a fireproof building in which this enormous tragedy occurred. Save for the three stories of blackened windows at the top, you would scarcely have been able to tell where the fire had happened. The walls stood firmly. A thin tongue of flame now and then licked around a window sash. . . .

On the ledge of a ninth-story window two girls stood silently watching the arrival of the first fire apparatus. Twice one of the girls made a move to jump. The other restrained her, tottering in her foothold as she did so. They watched firemen rig the ladders up against the wall.

They saw the last ladder lifted and pushed into place. They saw that it reached only the seventh floor.

For the third time, the more frightened girl tried to leap. The bells of arriving fire wagons must have risen to them. The other girl gesticulated in the direction of the sounds. But she talked to ears that could no longer hear. Scarcely turning, her companion dived head first into the street.

The other girl drew herself erect. The crowds in the street were stretching their arms up at her shouting and imploring her not to leap. She made a steady gesture, looking down as if to assure them she would remain brave.

But a thin flame shot out of the window at her back and touched her hair. In an instant her head was aflame. She tore at her burning hair, lost her balance, and came shooting down upon the mound of bodies below.

From opposite windows spectators saw again and again pitiable companionships formed in the instant of death—girls who placed their arms around each other as they leaped. In many cases their clothing was flaming or their hair flaring as they fell. . . .

By eight o'clock the available supply of coffins had been exhausted, and those that had already been used began to come back from the morgue. By that time bodies were lowered at the rate of one a minute, and the number of patrol wagons became inadequate, so that four, sometimes six, coffins were loaded upon each.

At intervals throughout the night the very horror of their task overcame the most experienced of the policemen and morgue attendants at work under the moving finger of the searchlight. The crews were completely changed no less than three times.

12

CHICAGO SUNDAY TRIBUNE

Thrilling Incidents in Gotham Holocaust That Wiped Out One Hundred and Fifty Lives

March 28, 1911

According to newspapers in small towns and large cities, popular interest in the fire was unusually intense, and readers pored over every detail of the tragedy. This story conveys the chaos and horror of the Triangle disaster and describes in sensational language the workers' struggles to survive the fire. The article, like many others in the United States, referred to New York by its nickname "Gotham," a term borrowed from a mythical English town populated by "wise fools."

In the office buildings across Washington place scores of men detained beyond office hours worked at their desks. One of them saw a girl rush to a window and throw up the sash. Behind her danced a seething curtain of yellow flame.

She climbed to the sill, stood in black outline against the light, hesitating, then, with a last touch of futile thrift, slipped her chatelaine bag over her wrist and jumped. Her body went whirling downward through the woven wire glass of a canopy to the flagging below.

Her sisters who followed flamed through the air like rockets. Their path could be followed but hardly heard.

It was eighty-five feet from the eighth floor to the ground, about ninety-five feet from the ninth floor, 115 feet from the cornice of the roof, and the upward rush of the draft and the crackle of the flames drowned their cries.

"Jimmy" Lehan, a traffic squad policeman, dashed up eight flights of stairs when the fire was at its height, braced his shoulders against a barred door, and burst it in. He found a score of girls mad with fright. He ordered them down the smoke filled stairways, but they balked.

From "Thrilling Incidents in Gotham Holocaust That Wiped Out One Hundred and Fifty Lives," *Chicago Sunday Tribune*, March 28, 1911, p. 2.

He used his club, and beat them down to safety. Not one of the number perished.

A boy who jumped from one of the upper floors was caught by a policeman who braced himself and held the youngster, practically uninjured, although both fell to the street.

Six girls fought their way to a window on the ninth floor over the bodies of fallen fellow workers and crawled out in single file to an eight inch stone ledge running the length of the building.

More than a hundred feet above the sidewalk they crept along their perilous pathway to a swinging electric feed wire spanning Washington place.

The leaders paused for their companions to catch up at the end of the ledge and the six grabbed the wire simultaneously. It snapped like rotten whipcord and they crashed down to death.

A 13 year old girl hung for three minutes by her finger tips to the sill of a tenth floor window. A tongue of flame licked at her fingers and she dropped into a life net held by firemen. Two women fell into the net at almost the same moment. The strands parted and the two were added to the death list.

A girl threw her pocketbook, then her hat, then her furs from a tenth floor window. A moment later her body came whirling after them to death.

At a ninth floor window a man and a woman appeared. The man embraced the woman and kissed her. Then he hurled her to the street and jumped. Both were killed.

Five girls smashed a pane of glass, dropped in a struggling tangle, and were crushed into a shapeless mass.

A girl on the eighth floor leaped for a firemen's ladder which reached only to the sixth floor. She missed, struck the edge of a life net, and was picked up with her back broken.

From one window a girl of about 13 years, a woman, a man, and two women with their arms about one another threw themselves to the ground in rapid succession. The little girl was whirled to the New York hospital in an automobile.

She screamed as the driver and a policeman lifted her into the hallway. A surgeon came out, gave one look at her face and touched her wrist.

"She is dead," he said.

One girl jumped into a horse blanket held by firemen and policemen. The blanket ripped like cheesecloth and her body was mangled almost beyond recognition.

Another dropped into a tarpaulin held by three men. Her weight tore it from their grasp and she struck the street, breaking almost every bone in her body.

Almost at the same time a man somersaulted down upon the shoulder of a policeman holding the tarpaulin. He glanced off, struck the sidewalk, and was picked up dead.

Within the building a man on the eighth floor stationed himself at the door of one of the elevators and with a club kept back the girls who had stampeded to the wire cage. Thirty were admitted to the car at a time. They were rushed down as fast as possible.

The call for ambulances was followed by successive appeals for police until 500 patrolmen arrived to cope with a crowd numbering tens of thousands—a mixture of the morbidly curious and of half crazed relatives and friends of the victims. A hundred mounted policemen had to charge the crowd repeatedly to keep it back.

Led by Fire Chief Croker, a squad of firemen stormed the stairways and gained access to the building at 7 o'clock. Two searchlights from buildings opposite lighted the way of the fire fighters as they ascended to the top floors.

Fifty roasted bodies were found on the ninth floor. They lay in every possible posture, some so charred that recognition was impossible. A half dozen were nude, with the flesh hanging in shreds to the bones.

Women with their hair burned away, with here and there a limb burned entirely off, and the charred stump visible, were lifted tenderly from the debris, wrapped in oilcloth, and lowered by pulleys to the street.

Across the street there rested on the sidewalk a hundred pine coffins, into which were placed the bodies. As fast as this was done the coffins were carried away in any kind of a vehicle that could be pressed into service to the morgue at Bellevue hospital and to the Charities Pier morgue. . . .

One of the first physicians on the scene was Dr. Ralph A. Froelich, 110 Waverley place. He saw most of the girls jump to the street, and as each one fell he rushed to her side and administered hypodermic injections to deaden the pain. He treated twelve of the victims, whom he found still breathing, but each died within a short time.

13

THE NEW YORK TIMES

Partners' Account of the Disaster

March 26, 1911

In this interview on the day of the fire, owners Max Blanck and Isaac Harris insisted that all proper precautions had been taken in the factory to prevent such a tragedy and that the doors were "always unlocked."

Max Blanck went to the home of his partner, Isaac Harris, at 324 West 101st Street, last night, and there told his story of what happened.

Two of his six children and their governess had come to visit him at the factory yesterday afternoon, and he was so shaken with the terror of the moments when it looked as if he and they would share the fate of the screaming hundreds he knew were perishing on the lower floors that it was only a fragmentary account he could give of the minutes before he and the children found their way to safety.

Mr. Blanck is an average type of the successful business man— short, stocky, and unemotional; but he sat in the reception room of his partner's home last night barely able to hold himself together while he answered questions. His partner, Harris, with his right hand bandaged

From "Partners' Account of the Disaster," *New York Times*, March 26, 1911, p. 4.

from injuries received while he was helping some of his employes to safety, paced the room and occasionally interjected facts.

Mr. Blanck's six children are all under 13 years of age. His wife and four of the children went to Florida for their health some weeks ago. Yesterday Henrietta, the oldest, and Mildred, 5 years old, went with their French governess, Mlle. Ehresmann, to their father's office, and were waiting to accompany him home when the fire began. Mr. Blanck said that he was waiting for a taxicab when he heard first a rumble of voices, and then shrill screams, which seemed to come from the street.

Panic Soon Began

He ran to the front windows, looked out, and saw upturned faces through a haze of smoke drifting out from the second floor below. He threw open the door to the front stairway and met one of his employes running up yelling, "Fire!" His voice was almost drowned in a roar from the hundreds of girls and men, who were already beginning to pile into the stairway.

Fearing that it would not be possible to take his children out that way, Mr. Blanck ran for the rear, but as soon as the rear doors to the stairway were opened the rush of heat and smoke drove back the throng of thirty bookkeepers, clerks, and operators who shared the tenth floor with the offices of the partners. It was then that the first elevator which had answered the frantic pushing of the tenth floor button appeared at that level.

Mr. Blanck had marshalled his children and the governess in the private office, and he and his partner were endeavoring to get the panic-stricken operators into some order. They had separated the men and women, and with the help of the bookkeepers managed to squeeze about ten women into the passenger elevator and get the door closed.

The elevator never came up again as far as Mr. Blanck could tell last night. The smoke and heat were becoming suffocating on the tenth floor by that time, and Mr. Blanck turned to his office, to find his two children and the governess out on the window sill.

He was about to join them when he heard the voice of his partner Harris shouting from the rear:

"The roof! Follow me to the roof!"

Blanck and the office force who were gathered in the private office with the children and the governess groped their way north through the smoke-filled sample room to a stairway boxed off near the centre of the building. The door was open and Harris had gone through pushing a group of the frightened operators before him.

Guarded His Children

Blanck kept his children out of the crush and sent the remaining office force and clerks up a stairway before he went himself. A salesman, E. T. Tischner, who was about to start on a trip and had come to the office to pack his sample cases was in a state of collapse from panic and Blanck and his bookkeeper stopped to help him up the stairway. The smoke and heat were so great behind them that it seemed the fire had finally burst into the tenth floor.

On the roof Harris took the lead and marshaled the women, pushing them toward the northeast corner of the building, where it joins a factory building at Wooster Street and Waverley Place. This building adjoins the rear of the Triangle Waist Company's factory for only about one-quarter of its length. The rest of the way to the westward the two buildings are separated from each other by a narrow well, for part of its length only ten feet wide. This was spouting flames and embers, which rained on the roof, and swirling eddies of hot gases added to the peril. . . .

Ladders were let down from its roof to the roof of the Triangle Waist Building and many of the girls and men were carried up. It was about fifteen feet higher, and the ladders were crowded with fighting, jostling girls and men, who most of the time were showered with sparks and choked with hot gases, but it is believed all escaped either to the American Book Company Building or the Waverley Place factory.

Blanck told his story in disconnected sentences, chiefly in response to questions and was hazy as to who had escaped with him, except his children and their governess. He remembered that his niece, Esther Harris, 18 years old, a bookkeeper on the ninth floor, had been badly burned, and sent to one of the hospitals, but was not sure how she escaped.

He also remembered that Diana Lipschitz of 405 Miller Avenue, Brooklyn, had been asked for in the throng in the street, but neither he nor his partner had any account of her. He remembered, too, that a shipping clerk named Smith had been one of those who got up to the roof, but in his state of nervous collapse could not name any others of the eighty who were waiting for the machinery to stop when the fire began.

Harris, who was pacing up and down with his wife during most of the interview, nursing his injured hand, told something of the escape, but he was most interested in explaining the precautions which the partners had taken to avoid just what had happened.

Harris Led Them to the Roof

. . . Blanck was asked what precautions he had taken about fire and what were the means of escape. He said the Building Department and factory Inspectors had all passed his lofts. . . .

Second Fire in the Building

Nine years ago, while the factory occupied but one floor of the building, there was a fire at night. Since then, Blanck said, he had employed a watchman night and day to look out for violations of the rules. One of the recognized dangers from fire was sparks from the motors. Since the factory has occupied three floors of the building— for the past three years—they have had seven motors most of the time in use.

Mr. Blanck said that as an extra precaution to avoid fire danger from the sparking of armatures he employed two negro engineers whose duties were to keep the motors in order, and two extra armatures were constantly kept in stock so as to have perfect apparatus always at hand in case a machine should get to sparking. Four of these motors were on the ninth floor, where most of the machines and about 350 operators were employed, and two of them were on the eighth floor, where about 300 operators were working yesterday.

The eighth floor is the main cutting room, and Mr. Blanck, in answer to questions, seemed to think that it was here that the fire might easily have started. He said that there was a large stock of material on this floor, most of it cut into shapes and piled up in stacks ready for the machines.

He also admitted that this material, being mostly lawns and other light cotton goods, was of a highly inflammable nature, and in the sewing rooms, where the flimsy stuff was being basted together and made ready for the operators, there must have been great stacks of fluffy material lying about on the machines.

Neither Mr. Blanck nor Mr. Harris could tell anything definite about the origin of the fire. They admitted under questioning that it was their belief that it started probably in the rear of the building and on their premises, although they said they believed all of the building was occupied except the sixth floor, from which the tenants were moving out.

The rear stairway was cut off at the tenth floor by smoke and flame, while the front stairway and front elevator were still running. Both partners agreed that they saw no elevators reach the tenth floor.

Fire Escapes Cut Off

As for the fire escapes, which were on the rear of the building and in a narrow well, there was never any time after the partners left their private office when escape was possible that way. Mr. Blanck said that when he reached the roof the entire well between his premises and the rear of the Waverly Place buildings seemed a roaring furnace with flames and glowing embers leaping high above the roof. He did not think that any one on either the eighth, ninth or tenth floors could have escaped that way.

Mr. Blanck was asked about the elevator service and the stairways. He said that as nearly as he could calculate the two front elevators, which were used all day long for passengers, easily carried ten passengers each. The two freight elevators in the rear were of iron construction and were also used as passenger elevators morning and evening when work began and ended. These, he said, would carry twenty persons each. The elevator boys on the freight elevators were accustomed to carry passengers during the rush period morning and evening each day. . . .

He repeated over and over again that he knew the doors into the hallway were always unlocked. He said that the keys were tied to the knobs and that he made it his personal duty every morning to go to each door and see that it was open. . . .

After the shirtwaist strike of last Summer the Harris & Blanck factories were about the first to start up and, in fact, Mr. Blanck said the Waverley Place lifts were the second in the city to resume work. At that time every demand of the strikers' committees had been complied with, but the only improvements which they had to ask for were additional accommodations in the women's dressing rooms.

It was only two days ago, Mr. Blanck said, that he had made an inspection of the entire premises and saw that all the fire buckets, of which there were 100, were full of water. This water was ordered changed every other day, so as to make sure that the buckets were kept full. There was also a fire alarm box on each floor.

Mr. Blanck could not remember whether it was the Building Department or the Fire Department which had last inspected the place, but he said that about eight days ago an official from some city department had been through the premises and reported everything perfect.

He said he believed the stock was worth about $200,000, but neither he nor his partner could be sure how much the insurance aggregated.

Unless the payroll was put in the safe on the tenth floor in the afternoon, the partners explained, the full roster of the dead may not be known. The only other records of the 700 employes were kept on card indexes on the several floors where they worked. These cards contained the names and addresses as well. The payroll contained only the names.

The card indexes were undoubtedly destroyed, both partners agreed, and they thought it extremely doubtful that the payroll had been put in the safe. It was pay day and the payroll was in use. In the ordinary course of routine the bookkeeper would have had it on his desk until the closing hour.

14

ROSEY SAFRAN

The Washington Place Fire

April 20, 1911

A Jewish immigrant from Austria, Rosey Safran had been in the United States for only one year when she joined the ILGWU and played an important role in the 1909 shirtwaist strike. Like many of her co-workers at Triangle, she made a connection between their failure to win union recognition and the fire of 1911. Working on the eighth floor that day, she was able to escape the flames, only to watch her friends perish.

From Rosey Safran, "The Washington Place Fire," *The Independent* LXX (April 20, 1911): 840–41.

This article was obtained by a representative of The Independent, who interviewed Miss Safran shortly after the disastrous fire in Washington place, New York City, March 25, 1911. An investigation by the Grand Jury has followed, and last week Isaac Harris and Max Blanck, owners of the Triangle Waist Company, were indicted for manslaughter in the first and second degrees, the maximum penalties being twenty and ten years' imprisonment, respectively. The partners are now under $25,000 bail.
—EDITOR [Hamilton Holt].

I, with a number of other girls, was in the dressing room on the eighth floor of the Asch Building, in Washington place, at 4.40 o'clock on the afternoon of Saturday, March 25, when I heard somebody cry "Fire!" I left everything and ran for the door on the Washington place side. The door was locked and immediately there was a great jam of girls before it. The fire was on the other side, driving us away from the only door that the bosses had left open for us to use in going in or out. They had the doors locked all the time for fear that some of the girls might steal something. At the one open door there was always a watchman who could see if any one carried out a bundle or if there was a suspicious lump in any one's clothing.

The fire had started on our floor and quick as I had been in getting to the Washington place door the flames were already blazing fiercely and spreading fast. If we couldn't get out we would all be roasted alive. The locked door that blocked us was half of wood; the upper half was thick glass. Some girls were screaming, some were beating the door with their fists, some were trying to tear it open. There were seven hundred of us girls employed by the Triangle Waist Company, which had three floors, the eighth, ninth and tenth, in the Asch Building. On our floor alone were two hundred and thirty. Most of us were crazy with fear and there was great confusion. Some one broke out the glass part of the door with something hard and heavy—I suppose the head of a machine—and I climbed or was pulled thru the broken glass and ran downstairs to the sixth floor, where some one took me down to the street.

I got out to the street and watched the upper floors burning, and the girls hanging by their hands and then dropping as the fire reached up to them. There they were dead on the sidewalk. It was an awful, awful sight, especially to me who had so many friends among the girls and young men who were being roasted alive or dashed to death. I can't describe how I felt as I stood there watching. I could see the figures, but not the faces—the police kept us all too far back. We hoped that the fire nets would save some, but they were no good for persons falling so far. One girl broke thru the thick glass in the sidewalk and fell down into a cellar. That shows with what force they came down from the ninth floor.

One girl jumped from the ninth floor and her clothing caught on a hook that stuck out from the wall on the eighth. The fire burned thru her clothing and she fell to the sidewalk and was killed. Another girl fell from the eighth to the sixth floor, when a hook supporting a sign caught her clothes and held her. She smashed the window of the sixth floor with her fist and got in the shop and went down to the street, saving herself. One of my friends, Annie Rosen, was an examiner on the ninth floor. She was near a window when the cry of fire was raised. She tried to open the window to get out. It stuck, but she got it open and climbed on a little fire escape. The fire was coming up from the eighth floor and in getting from the ninth to the eighth her hat and her hair were burned. She doesn't know how she got to the eighth; maybe she fell. She was going to jump to the ground, but the people who were watching her from the street shouted not to do it, and somehow she got thru the flames. She fell from the eighth to the sixth floor on the fire escape and then she was carried down to the street and taken to Bellevue Hospital, where there were many of her companions. She is out now, but pale as a ghost; she does not think that she will ever be strong again. She has lost her nerve and is afraid all the time.

I was on the street with other girls watching. We were screaming for about twenty minutes and then some one took me home. I don't know who it was. Afterward I went to the Morgue and saw my friends there. Ida Jacobowski, Rosey Sorkin, Bennie Sklawer, Jacob Klein, Sam Lehrer and others. It was on the ninth floor that there was the great loss of life. Altogether 145 were killed and of these 120 belonged on the ninth floor. When firemen broke open the door on the Washington place side they found fifty bodies piled up there. I, who worked on the eighth floor, was unhurt, except for the shock, and will go to work again at the same business as soon as I can get a job in a fireproof factory.

I was in the great shirtwaist strike that lasted thirteen weeks. I was one of the pickets and was arrested and fined several times. The union paid my fines. Our bosses won and we went back to the Triangle Waist Company as an open shop having nothing to do with the union. But we strikers who were taken back stayed in the union, for it is our friend. If the union had had its way we would have been safe in spite of the fire, for two of the union's demands were, adequate fire escapes on factory buildings and open doors giving free access from factories to the street. The bosses defeated us and we didn't get the open doors or the large fire escapes, and so our friends are dead and relatives are tearing their hair.

In persuading us to go back to work after the strike the bosses showed us how easy it was to make good wages on the scale they offered. The waist styles then were simple, with little trimming. So we did make good wages at first. Then the styles changed to more complicated designing and more trimming, with the scale the same. We couldn't make so many of the shirt waists and so we didn't earn so much money. Our hours were from 7.30 in the morning till 6 in the evening, but we could work overtime if we liked and also could work on Sundays—making seven days' work a week. There was no extra pay for this overtime work. The bosses wanted us to do it when there was a rush of business, but they would not pay any higher rate. Generally, overtime is paid for at a higher rate. I averaged about $14 a week. I worked overtime at that. Sometimes I made $18 a week. That is the most earned by the smartest girl and that means working from 7.30 in the morning till 9 o'clock at night and Sundays too.

I learned to operate a machine in Chlebowice, Galicia, Austria, where I was born. Chlebowice is a little country village. I came to this country three years ago, and for the last two and a half years till the date of the fire I worked for the Triangle Waist Company. The wages were not so bad, tho many of the girls only made $6 and $8 a week, but they should have had some regard for our lives.

15

THE NEW YORK TIMES

120,000 Pay Tribute to the Fire Victims
April 6, 1911

Fearing riots and revolution, Mayor Gaynor refused to release the seven unidentified bodies to either the WTUL or the ILGWU, explaining that the city would handle their burials. But the union and the WTUL decided to hold a funeral procession for the unclaimed victims in order to show solidarity and respect for the fallen. Some 350,000 people took part in the funeral march; 120,000 walked the entire route through the city streets,

From "120,000 Pay Tribute to Fire Victims," *New York Times*, April 6, 1911, p. 1.

and at least another 400,000 watched the parade of mourners as they passed by. Black bunting draped city buildings, and working- and middle-class women, also dressed in black, clung to each other as they remembered their "sisters."

Rose Schneiderman, the slip of a girl whose eloquence stirred the Metropolitan Opera House mass meeting on Sunday, brought tears to the eyes of thousands yesterday as they stood along Fifth Avenue in a drifting rain, watching the funeral parade for the shirtwaist workers who perished in the Washington Place fire.

Little Miss Schneiderman had made many speeches since the Asch Building fire: workers everywhere had become acquainted with her. Hatless and without raincoat she tried to trudge along in the dripping procession, near its head. But long before it had reached its uptown destination at Thirty-fifth Street her feet began to falter.

Mary Dreier, President of the Women's Trade Union League, noticed that the girl was lagging behind her comrades in a line of eight, and took hold of her arm. Helen Marot, Secretary of the league, grasped her by the other arm, and the three, who more than any others have been in the limelight since the Asch Building fire, trudged on. None had umbrellas, and only one a raincoat. In front of them was a platoon of police, a funeral car laden with floral wreaths, with six white horses to draw it, and a score of fire survivors one of whom carried a waistmakers' banner.

The crowds, which numbered, the police estimated, about 400,000, while a third of that number were in the line of march, everywhere recognized the girl who was being helped along. Her name ran from lip to lip along the curb lines. Men pressed close to catch a glimpse of her, and among the women, who outnumbered the men on the sidewalks as they did in the line of march, there were few dry eyes.

The parade, declared by the leaders to be the largest demonstration ever made here by working people, practically emptied the downtown and Brooklyn lofts and factories. Its numbers were at first largely underestimated, as it was thought the rain would keep most of the paraders away. But when, an hour later than the scheduled time for starting, a squad of traffic policemen headed into Washington Square from the south side, and another squad took its place on the northern edge, with a line of drenched paraders stretching out behind in both directions, estimators began to revise their figures. From 10,000, at which they started, they raised the figures to 100,000, and then to 120,000.

Difficulties of getting through crowded downtown streets and passing fire lines drawn about a burning building had detained the downtown section, which worked its way up to Washington Square from Rutgers Square, arriving at 3 o'clock instead of 2 as planned. Similar troubles had delayed the uptown section which had formed at Fourth Avenue and Twenty-second Street. Once in Washington Square, the consolidated columns began the march up Fifth Avenue at 3:40 o'clock, and it required four hours after the first file of eight had left for the last file to pass under the Washington Arch.

There were no propagandist banners and no bands. The intention of the leaders to make the occasion one for the expression of the working people's grief was complied with, but only by the rigid censorship of banners which some had brought to the line of procession. The National colors, draped in mourning, and union banners similarly draped, marked the headquarters of the various divisions. Girls, where the unions were composed of women, carried their banners throughout the line of march, and then would not admit that they were exhausted. On their hats and around their arms many wore bands of black ribbon.

At Thirty-fifth Street the parade turned into Fourth Avenue and then continued to Madison Square, where they dispersed, every parader thoroughly drenched by the drifting rain and mist.

While the parade was in progress a funeral procession, consisting of eight black hearses, with white trimmings, carrying the bodies of six unidentified women and a man, left the Morgue, at the foot of East Twenty-sixth Street. Thousands of people who had been attracted by the funeral notice watched the procession on its way to the Twenty-third Street ferries, and thousands more from Brownsville lined the streets through which the procession passed from the Brooklyn ferry slip to the Cypress Hills Cemetery.

Inspector Sweeney, from Brooklyn, and a force of seventy-five men were out to see that there was no disorder. . . .

Mrs. Raymond Robins of Chicago, National President of the Women's Trade Union League, was a marcher in the parade. She had come from Chicago especially to participate in it. With her was Leonora O'Reilly, who is to have charge of the factory inspections on which demands for specific changes looking to better fire protection are to be based.

Just behind the league officials marched the suffragists and suffragettes, and then came the Socialists. Of the suffragists there was one who wore a conspicuously elaborate gown and carried a pink umbrella. She marched with the uptown section to Washington Square, and then, while waiting for the consolidation of the two lines, she deserted. Mrs. Harriet Stanton Blatch marched the entire route at the expense of her gown, and with her marched Dr. Helen Knight, Mrs. Sophia Kramer, Mrs. Jeanette Rankin, Mrs. John Rodgers, and many others of the various suffragist organizations.

Through the east side, where sympathy with the "silent parade" was most tense, handkerchiefs waved from windows on both sides of the streets. In Fifth Avenue the only drapings observed were on the Church of the Ascension, whose doors were hung with American flags and crepe.

While thousands of mourners were gathered at the graves in Cypress Hills Cemetery, Brooklyn, in which the unidentified bodies of seven victims of the Asch Building fire were buried, Brownsville's grief was evinced by the closing of all clothing factories, a parade in which 5,000 girls and men took part, and several memorial meetings.

16

REPORT OF THE RED CROSS EMERGENCY RELIEF COMMITTEE OF THE CHARITY ORGANIZATION OF THE SOCIETY OF THE CITY OF NEW YORK

Emergency Relief after the Washington Place Fire: New York, March 25, 1911

1912

The Triangle fire mobilized the public and private agencies of the city. The Red Cross and the ILGWU organized to provide relief to the victims' families. Within days, the Red Cross, in cooperation with the municipal charity association, raised over $100,000 in relief funds and then terminated the campaign, rejecting additional donations as unnecessary. Concerned about providing too much relief and explaining that it did not

From Red Cross Emergency Relief Committee, *Emergency Relief after the Washington Place Fire, New York, March 25, 1911: A Report* (New York: The Committee, 1912), 20–21, 27, 37–38.

want to foster dependence, the Red Cross doled out only $80,000 of the funds received. The goal, according to Red Cross officials, was to assist those in need of immediate aid and help families that had relied on the victims' wages become independent again. Volunteers visited every family that requested aid and conducted thorough investigations before releasing any money. By applying the principle of attempting to restore families to their former standard of living, the Red Cross allotted more aid to the families of workers who had earned more money. Accordingly, the families of male victims received considerably more assistance than did those who had relied on the meager wages of women workers.

No. 120. (Russian.) A man, 30 years old, was killed, leaving a wife and two children, four and two years of age. They had been in this country only three months. The woman spoke no English and had no trade and had no near relatives in this country except a sister who had come over with her and was almost as helpless. After the fire she went to a poor cousin, whose family was seriously incommoded by the addition of four people. She wished to return to Russia, where she had a brother and a sister. Her passage was engaged, passport and other official papers were secured, arrangements made for having her looked after at all points in Russia where she would change cars, and for paying to her a lump sum of money with which to establish a business. Three days before she was to sail, however, she received a letter from her brother telling her on no account to return, as there were rumors of pogroms[1] and of a foreign war. This so frightened her that she was not willing to go. A few days later she again changed her mind and wished to go home. Arrangements were again made for her return, and again, a day or two before the date of sailing, she refused to go. The United Hebrew Charities was then requested to take charge of the family. $1050.00 altogether has been placed with that society to be used in current expenses and in carrying out some plan for making the woman self-supporting; and $4000.00 to be kept as a trust fund for the two little children.   ($5,167.20)

No. 18. (Russian.) A man, 27 years old, was killed, leaving a wife and a baby of 11 months. He had earned good wages, $14.00–$20.00 per week. The wife—young, apparently intelligent but without knowledge

---

[1]*pogroms*: violence directed against a certain ethnic or religious group, particularly Jews.

of English—was for several weeks hysterically anxious to get her plans for the future settled. She went from one office to another to get advice as to what she could do to support herself. At first she wanted to be established in a stationery store, but it soon appeared that her health had suffered so seriously from the shock that she was not in condition to undertake anything. Through the summer her expenses were paid in the country. In November she was still unable to work, in the opinion of a physician who gave her a careful examination, and she seemed to have lost her ambition to become self-supporting. A monthly allowance is being paid through the winter and at the end of that time it is expected that her health will be restored and she will be able to take up some occupation. She is under the care of the United Hebrew Charities, who have advised in regard to her from the first. $320.00 was expended up to November; $1000.00 was then sent to the United Hebrew Charities for further living expenses and to establish the woman in business when her health is restored; and $2000.00 was placed with that society as a trust fund for the child.   ($3,320.00)

No. 96. (Italian.) A girl of 18 was incapacitated by nervous shock. She is the second of four children and her mother is a widow. Her older sister is not strong and therefore does not work regularly. On the recommendation of the Brooklyn Bureau of Charities $250.00 was placed with them to be used as a pension while the girl was not able to work. In October she was entirely recovered and three of the four children were working, earning together $20.00 a week. Later the girl returned to the employ of the Triangle Shirt Waist Company at her former wages.   ($250.00)

No. 203. (Italian.) A girl of 22, the only wage-earner in a family of seven, incapacitated by the shock. The father was ill, in need of surgical treatment which he would not consent to have. The family was placed under the care of the Charity Organization Society, and the girl was sent to the country, but she stayed only half a day at the first place to which she was sent and six days at the second. $250.00 was sent to the Charity Organization Society for the benefit of the family. In October the girl was well and at work, but still nervous about working in a factory. The father was also working regularly, but had not yet been persuaded to have the needed operation.   ($255.81)

No. 218. (Russian.) A girl of 22, the only support of her mother and young brother, incapacitated for some time by the shock. $325.00 was given through the Brooklyn Bureau of Charities.   ($325.00)

No. 52. (Italian.) A widow of 28, seriously injured. At the time of the accident her 13-year-old daughter was living with her, and her two little boys were in an institution. $127.50 was given in April in the expectation that this would be sufficient to meet the needs of the family until the woman should be able to work. In August she applied for the commitment of her two boys who had returned to her in June, and in consequence of this the family came under the care of the Charity Organization Society. Later, as the woman's health was found to be still seriously affected in consequence of the fire, an additional grant of $200.00 was placed with the Charity Organization Society for her benefit. This amount was based upon the recommendations and prognosis of a reliable physician.   ($327.50)

No. 145. (Italian.) A girl of 17, not injured and back at work within a week. No assistance seemed to be needed at the time of the fire, but in October it was found that she had not been able to replace the winter clothing which she had lost in the fire, and $50.00 was accordingly given to her to meet this need.   ($50.00)

No. 208. (Italian.) A girl of 20, the only support of her mother and two younger sisters, slightly incapacitated by nervousness. The father was in Italy, sick, and an older daughter was with him. This girl still had $2.00 of her savings left when she asked for help a month after the fire.   ($50.00)

No. 211. (Italian.) A girl of 19, temporarily incapacitated. She was living with her brother's family and sent money regularly to her father in Italy. $50.00 was given on April 26 and an offer was made to arrange for a week in the country but this was not accepted.   ($50.00)

No. 220. (Russian.) A girl of 18, incapacitated by cut hand and hysterical condition, asked for help by sending an affidavit six weeks after the fire. She lived with her mother and three brothers and sisters, two of whom were employed at good wages. $50.00 was given through the United Hebrew Charities to enable her to go to the country. In November it was reported that her health was restored and the family income was $37.00 per week.   ($50.00)

No. 210. (Italian.) A girl of 18, the principal support of her father and mother, anæmic and suffering from nervous shock. $50.00 was given in order that she might go to the country. She would stay only six days because she wanted to be at home to see her sister start for Italy.   ($55.81)

17

ELIZABETH DUTCHER

Budgets of the Triangle Fire Victims

September 1912

In so many ways, the "girl" shirtwaist makers surprised the citizens of New York. They defied popular notions about women, work, and trade unionism. Newspaper and local leaders had marveled at their steadfastness during the 1909 strike, their courage on the picket line, despite their youth, and the significant financial roles they assumed in their families. But employers often dismissed them as temporary workers, waiting for marriage and working for "spending money" to satisfy their personal— and unnecessary—consumer wants. The investigations made by the Red Cross after the fire, however, shattered that myth. WTUL member Elizabeth Dutcher served on the relief committees of both the Red Cross and the ILGWU and found that these women workers were economically essential to the welfare of their families. Her findings initially appeared in The Woman Voter *and were reprinted by the WTUL in its monthly publication,* Life and Labor.

It is now over a year since the terrible fire in the Triangle shirt-waist factory in Washington Place, where one hundred and forty-six people lost their lives, and many more were injured. The large relief fund of $120,000, which was at once raised to meet the needs of the sufferers, was dispersed after unusually careful and searching investigations made by the relief organizations, the Red Cross Committee and the Joint Relief Committee of the Ladies' Waist Makers' Union. Some of the families required long, continued care in the process of adjustment after the shock, and the final reports of the relief committees are just being made public. These reports are detailed, and because they give the fact so fully, and because most of the cases are concerned with the problem of one young working woman, they are of very unusual interest.

From Elizabeth Dutcher, "Budgets of the Triangle Fire Victims," *Life and Labor*, September 1912, 265–67.

There are still many people who secretly believe that women come into industry in a very casual way; that they are not earnest about it; that their chief desire is to obtain through it extra spending money; and that men are their natural protectors, who stand between them and the stern realities, and accordingly represent them in the public life of the country. To all of us, perhaps, these budgets come as a shock, and bring a revelation.

* * * The women who jumped from the tenth story of the Asch Building were self-reliant working women, who had never asked for charitable assistance,[1] and who were making their way in the average fashion—or a little above the average, for the strain of work in this particular factory was very great, and capable women, of good physique, who could be speeded up, and work overtime during the busy season, were sought after by the employers.

They lived mostly on the East side and on the lower West side, though some lived in Harlem and in the tenement districts of Brooklyn. They were working in a seasonal industry where there was no work for four months, light work for about three months, and very heavy work with a great deal of overtime[2] during the remaining five months. The fire occurred late one Saturday afternoon in March, at the close of the busy season, when overtime was still being worked, and the pay-envelopes for that week ranged from $4.50 to $14, with an exceptional few still higher.

What is the first statement made in the report of the Red Cross Committee? Says that report:

"The families affected by the Washington Place fire were for the most part Jewish and Italian immigrants . . . dependent largely on the earnings of girls and women."

These girls, then, just at the age when clothes and good times make their greatest appeal, were not working at a power machine in a high loft building for nothing. They were there because they were the support of a great number of people.

The Red Cross Committee, with its 166 cases makes the statement we have just quoted. I want to illustrate just how this support was given

---

[1] P. 7 Report of the Red Cross Emergency Relief Committee: "These were for the most part families who had never received charitable assistance." This is the more remarkable because one in every nine families in New York receive some form of charity every year. Only one of the sixty-five union families had so received aid. [Dutcher's note]

[2] Overtime is legal three nights in the week, but the charge has been made that four nights were commonly worked in this shop, and even Sundays and holidays in time of stress. [Dutcher's note]

by giving you some figures from the union records, partly because I am more familiar with them, and partly because they are the families where such heavy responsibilities seem most improbable. One would not expect one girl whose young shoulders carried such heavy burdens to run the risk of a long strike, or to make the sacrifices necessary for paying her union dues and assessments, particularly when she was working in a non-union shop, where organization was discouraged in every possible way.[3]

Sixty-five cases were taken for continued care by the Joint Relief Committee. These included families where one or more members had been killed or injured in the disaster, and there was some union connection.

Of these sixty-five Jewish and Italian families sixty-two of the victims were girls or women (four families having two women victims each; seven families having men victims only):

(a) *Fifteen* gave practically all their salary *toward* the support of families living in America.

(b) *Nineteen*[4] were the *whole* or *main* support (that is, providing more than one-half of the weekly income) of families living in America. Of these *three* were married, and supported idle husbands, as well as their children, and partly supported aged parents, and *four*[5] were the heads of families, in the sense that they had younger brothers and sisters living with them as dependents, and no older people.

(c) *Twenty-one* sent sums ranging from $5 to $20 per month (verified in all cases by money order receipts), to dependents living in Russia, Austria, Italy and Palestine.

(d) *Twenty-one* were either alone in New York (without any member of their immediate family in the city), or two sisters were alone and lived and worked together.[6]

The average age was about nineteen years. . . .

These girls in their teens—typical New York working women—were supporting old fathers and mothers, both in this country and abroad; mothering and supporting younger brothers and sisters, sending

---

[3]This was of course the shop where the trouble started, and which was out the longest in the shirtwaist strike of 1909–10. The strikers were out five months, and were then compelled to settle on an open shop basis. Most of the union girls who went back were discharged shortly thereafter, and only three of the union cases were girls who had been in the strike. [Dutcher's note]

[4]In two instances two girls were together the main support of a household. [Dutcher's note]

[5]Of these one had an older brother who had never helped her in any way, living in another part of the city. [Dutcher's note]

[6]Of course there is considerable duplication in the above list, many girls under (d) coming also under (c). But note, there is no duplication between (a) and (b). [Dutcher's note]

brothers to high school, to art school, to dental college, to engineering courses.

Why is it so easy for the woman worker to get work, and why is she becoming more and more in some parts of our community, as these budgets show, the dependable family bread winner? The answer is not in her deftness alone; it is also her submissiveness and her cheapness. Women will submit to worse conditions, longer hours, and shorter wages than men. People have always said that this was because they were "only working for pin money,"—or (a grudging concession), that they "had only themselves to support." We have seen from the above what heavy responsibilities they in reality carry. Is the low wage, the submission, an inheritance from the days when the working girl was first edging timidly into industry, driven by her wants and glad to get any return for her day's work? Or is it that there is always in the back of the employer's mind, the sense of her sex-inferiority— the knowledge that she belongs to a group without political rights, who may be oppressed with impunity, and forced to underbid her own men-folks?

During the strike of 1909–10 the most frequent complaints were of excessive overtime (of which the greatest grievance was that it precluded night school), excessive speeding up, heavy fines, a subcontracting system which amounted to sweating within the factory, and low wages. It was the revolt of one of the sub-contractors that started the strike. Once it was under way, the girls began to realize their disabilities to the full. They received no protection from their natural protectors, those enforcing the laws of the city.

Special officers were placed at the doors of the factory to insult them as they picketed, and no policeman interfered; the picketing itself was declared illegal, and girls of fifteen were sent to the workhouse for picketing and shut up in the same cells with thieves and prostitutes. Magistrate Cornell's contemptuous pronouncement, "You have no right to picket, you have no right to be on Washington Place, if you go there you will get what is coming to you and I won't interfere," rang out as an expression of the law's typical attitude. It was not until a large number of the so-called "influential women," in other words, women who had assets of wealth and education, and therefore were least in need of such influence, came and picketed morning and night with the girls that there was any change in the law's attitude to these defenseless women.

That the strike involved great hardship every one who was with the girls recognized; though the girls were brave and uncomplaining,

one heard occasionally of a picket who had had nothing to eat all day,
or of another who found all her little possessions on the stairway—
dispossessed on her return from the long tramp. But the true significance of a five-months' strike comes with new force to the readers of
these Fire Disaster reports. Take Sarah R.[7] for instance. She was seventeen years old, and lived with her widowed stepmother and two little
brothers in a five-story double tenement. Her stepmother had rent free
in exchange for janitress work, work which she was too feeble to do
herself. So night times, after coming home, and in the early morning,
Sarah did all the cleaning of the great building. What is more, she
made all the clothes for the family, even the little brothers' suits. No
wonder her best friend said of her sorrowfully: "Sarah was a fine girl,
but no one ever knew her; she was too busy." Do you know any man
whose family are dependent on him to the same extent? . . .

The twenty-one girls who were sending money abroad all had interesting stories. Here is a typical one: Rose M. was killed. The only
other member of her family in New York was a brother nineteen years
old, who could barely support himself. Her father, in Russia, had with
him five other children, two of whom were hunchbacks. His employment in a forest brought only twelve roubles a month and the greater
part of the family budget in the last three years had been covered by
the 420 roubles which the daughter had sent in that time.

And so one could go on to tell of Violet M., who was supporting a
large family and yet insisting that the oldest brother should go on and
finish his high school course; . . . of a half dozen cases like Minnie R.,
so careful of appearances, "never forgetting to wear her puffs," as her
landlady, divided between pride and grief, told the visitor, and who had
brought her delicate little sister to this country and faced bravely the
problem of an uncertain seven dollars a week for two orphan girls
alone in New York. This, then, is the stuff out of which the great
strikes of the last few years have been made—the shirtwaist strike,
the cloak-makers' strike, the laundry workers' strike, the neckwear
makers' strike—the public has grown weary of strikes, and yet the
situation must be desperate indeed that forces women with such
heavy responsibilities to face not just their own suffering, but that of
those dearest to them through a long period.

[7]The cases given are from both the Red Cross and Union reports. In no instance is
the real name given. [Dutcher's note]

18

ROSE SCHNEIDERMAN

All for One

1967

In 1955 Rose Schneiderman began work on her autobiography, which was not completed until 1967. Publication was a controversial enterprise that left Schneiderman disappointed with the final version. Initially unable to find a publisher (she was told that Americans would not buy a book about a woman labor organizer), Schneiderman persuaded her union, the ILGWU, to buy five thousand copies in order to pay for the first printing.

In this excerpt, Schneiderman retells her call for justice after the Triangle fire—a passionate plea that riveted the audience, captured the attention of the New York Times, and led, according to Frances Perkins, to the establishment of the Factory Investigation Commission.

The day after the fire, while the lifeless bodies of the women were still being gathered from the charred debris, a special joint meeting of the executive boards of the League, the Shirtwaist Makers Union, and the Hebrew Trades was called by the League at its headquarters. A relief committee to cooperate with the Red Cross in its work among the families of the victims was formed, and another committee was appointed to broaden the investigation and research on fire hazards in New York factories which was already being carried on by the League.

The League also established and played a vital part in another committee, the New York City Citizens Committee on Safety. First, it called a mass meeting on May 2 to protest the lack of safety and the inhuman conditions in the factories. Through the generosity of Anne Morgan the meeting was held at the Metropolitan Opera House. There was not an empty seat by the time it began. Jacob Schiff, the well-known financier and philanthropist, was chairman. Among the speakers were eminent civic leaders, churchmen, lawyers, labor-union

From Rose Schneiderman with Lucy Goldthwaite, *All for One* (New York: Paul S. Eriksson, 1967), 99–102.

officials, and representatives of women's organizations. The latter included not so eminent me.

After Monsignor White, Bishop David H. Greer, Rabbi Stephen Wise, and E. R. A. Seligman, the well-known economist from Columbia University, had spoken, the meeting asked for the adoption of a resolution calling for the appointment of a fire-prevention bureau, more factory inspectors, and some sort of compensation for workmen. Many in the audience were tired of resolutions being passed but never acted upon. There were shouts and hisses from the galleries and interruptions from the floor. The meeting seemed doomed to break up in disorder.

Then it was my turn to speak. I was so overcome that I could hardly talk above a whisper, but for some reason in that huge auditorium my voice carried. I think I shall let the *New York Times* tell the rest of the story as it appeared in the paper the next day. I could never write a speech that amounted to anything. But once I got on the stage, the words poured out and I am grateful to the *Times* for preserving my words that night:

> ... There was one moment when feeling grew tense to a snapping point, and the audience was held too closely by the speaker's words to interrupt or applaud as the girl who had been speaking went back up the stage to her seat.
>
> Rose Schneiderman, who led the workers out of the Triangle factory in their strike two years ago and bailed them out after being arrested, found words difficult when she tried to speak. She stood silently for a moment and then began to speak hardly above a whisper. But the silence was such that everywhere they carried clearly.
>
> "I would be a traitor to these poor burned bodies," began Miss Schneiderman after she had gained possession of her voice, "If I came here to talk good fellowship. We have tried you good people of the public and we have found you wanting. The old Inquisition had its rack and its thumbscrews and its instruments of torture with iron teeth. We know what these things are today: the iron teeth are our necessities, the thumbscrews the high-powered and swift machinery close to which we must work, and the rack is here in the fire-proof structures that will destroy us the minute they catch on fire.
>
> "This is not the first time girls have been burned alive in the city. Every week I must learn of the untimely death of one of my sister workers. Every year thousands of us are maimed. The life of men and women is so cheap and property is so sacred. There are so many of us for one job it matters little if 143 of us are burned to death.

"We have tried you, citizens; we are trying you now, and you have a couple of dollars for the sorrowing mothers and daughters and sisters by way of a charity gift. But every time the workers come out in the only way they know to protest against conditions which are unbearable, the strong hand of the law is allowed to press down heavily upon us.

"Public officials have only words of warning to us—warning that we must be intensely orderly and must be intensely peaceable, and they have the workhouse just back of all their warnings. The strong hand of the law beats us back when we rise into the conditions that make life bearable.

"I can't talk fellowship to you who are gathered here. Too much blood has been spilled. I know from my experience it is up to the working people to save themselves. The only way they can save themselves is by a strong working-class movement."

The words that night were clear and strong enough to be heard all the way up to Albany.

19

MARTHA BENSLEY BRUERE

The Triangle Fire

May 1911

Socialite, reformer, and member of the WTUL, Martha Bensley Bruere had been overwhelmed by the tragedy of the fire and the public display of grief. From her window, she watched the funeral procession for the unidentified seven victims for six hours, noting "Never have I seen a military pageant or triumphant ovation so impressive." Bruere provided what many regarded as one of the most comprehensive overviews of the Triangle strike and fire and became best known for the question she raises in the essay: "Now what is going to be done about it?" That question helped catalyze a movement for reform and an attempt to put the Triangle owners in jail.

From Martha Bensley Bruere, "The Triangle Fire," *Life and Labor*, May 1911, 137–41.

The Triangle Shirt Waist Shop in New York City, which was the scene of the great fire on March 25th, when 143 workers were killed, was also the starting point of the strike of the forty-thousand shirt waist workers in 1909.

The girls struck because they wished to stand together for decent shop conditions, wages on which they could live and reasonable hours, and neither Mr. Harris nor Mr. Blanck, both of whom were members of the Manufacturers' Association, would allow their workers to unite in any way at all.

It happened that I did picket duty morning and night before that shop and saw the striking girls go up to the strikebreakers and ask timidly:

"Don't you know there's a strike by the Triangle?"

It was before this Triangle Shop that the girls were clubbed by the police and by the hired thugs who assisted them; and it was in the streets around it that a large number of arrests were made. The girl pickets were dragged to court, but every one from this shop was discharged. The police and the government of the city had banded themselves together to protect the property of Harris and Blanck, the Triangle Shirt Waist firm.

The six hundred girls who worked at the Triangle Shop were beaten in the strike. They had to go back without the recognition of the union and with practically no change in conditions. On the 25th of March it was these same policemen who had clubbed them and beaten them back into submission, who kept the thousands in Washington Square from tramping upon their dead bodies, sent for the ambulances to carry them away, and lifted them one by one into the receiving coffins which the Board of Charities sent down in wagon loads.

I was coming down Fifth Avenue on that Saturday afternoon when a great swirling, billowing cloud of smoke swept like a giant streamer out of Washington Square and down upon the beautiful homes in lower Fifth Avenue. Just as I was turning into the Square two young girls whom I knew to be working in the vicinity came rushing toward me, tears were running from their eyes and they were white and shaking as they caught me by the arm.

"Oh," shrieked one of them, "they are jumping."

"Jumping from ten stories up! They are going through the air like bundles of clothes and the firemen can't stop them and the policemen can't stop them and nobody can't help them at all!"

"Fifty of them's jumped already and just think how many there must be left inside yet"—and the girls started crying afresh and rushed away up Fifth Avenue.

A little old tailor whom I knew came shrieking across the Square, tossing his arms and crying, "Horrible, horrible." He did not recognize me, nor know where he was; he had gone mad with the sight. The minister of a fashionable church sank limp and white on one of the park benches and covered his face with his hands, unable to face the horror. For four blocks to the east the streets ran ankle deep with the water from the fire engines, and the crowd surged back and forth, breaking in repeated panics as ambulances and automobiles filled with injured and dead rushed through.

The police tried to keep the fire lines. The reserves were called out and formed into a cordon of blue backs against the surging crowd, but the Triangle shop was just on the edge of the quarter where live half a million Italians; the working day was over and thousands of factory workers were pouring into Washington Square on their way home, the mass of workers pressed in and in on the fire lines, and what can policemen do against a whole quarter mad with terror at seeing its sisters and daughters burned before its eyes? Can you quiet a man who thinks that the charred mass over which a merciful blanket has just been thrown, is his newly married wife? Sometimes the mob shrieked that the still forms on the pavement were not dead; sometimes they raged at the firemen because they did not do the impossible, for the extension ladders only reached to the sixth story, while the fire was on the eighth, ninth and tenth—the scaling ladders were useless— the girls jumped so rapidly and so many together that the life nets broke through, and as Battalion Chief Worth said afterward:

"There was no apparatus in the department which could have been of service."

The city government which, through its policemen and detectives had compelled the girls to go back to work at the Triangle Shop, was quite powerless to save their lives.

But why did the girls jump to death? Why did they wait and burn in their workrooms? Why didn't they leave the building? Said Sadie Bergida:

"We all ran for the Washington Place door. When we tried to open it we found it was locked. The flames were racing up behind us and the room was filled with smoke. We girls struggled desperately to force open the door; there was a snap lock on the inside, however, and it held till Mr. Brown, a machinist, ran up and throwing his body against the door, burst it open. But most of the girls by that time had rushed to the Greene Street door. Of what happened after that I have only a very faint recollection. It seems to me that I tumbled down the stairs to the street."

Said Tessa Benani:

"My sister Sarah and I worked alongside of each other and our cousin Josey worked a little ways off. We ran with about forty other girls to the Washington Place doors and found them locked, and we beat on those iron doors with our bare hands and tried to tear off the big padlock. The girls behind us were screaming and crying. Several of them, as the flames crept up closer, ran into the smoke, and we heard them scream as the flames caught their clothes. One little girl, who worked at the machine opposite me, cried out in Italian, "Good-bye, good-bye." I have not seen her since. My cousin Josey staggered through the mob and made direct for the flames. The next I heard of her was when they brought her body home from the morgue. She had jumped! Half a dozen other girls went into the flames that were eating up the Greene Street side. They all jumped from the windows."

Tessa and Sarah Benani also escaped when William Brown broke open the door.

Around the entrance to the freight elevator which the girls were expected to use was a partition with a narrow door through which the girls could only pass one at a time. Some of the girls did not even know of the existence of the passenger elevator reserved for officials of the firm, which might have saved them. There was a small stairway to the roof by which N. Harris and Blanck and a few of their relatives escaped; but I have been unable to discover that any of the employees even knew of its existence.

There were two reasons why these three natural exits, the doors to the stairway, the elevator, and the roof were obstructed; first, to guard against a sudden exodus of employees in concerted protest; second, to prevent the girls stealing anything. Said Ida Deutchman:

"This is the worst shop I ever worked in. When applying for work you must undergo a half hour examination about union affiliations. When a girl was hired, after working at the machine she would again be asked by the man in charge of the floor if she was a member of the Union. For the five months I worked in the shop I saw women come and go on account of the spy system they have.

"When leaving work they have men at the Greene Street door searching all the girls. We were made to open our pocketbooks, and when a girl didn't do it she was made to come up two or three flights and show that she didn't have a piece of lace or anything else. A girl could not carry a waist in her pocketbook, and all one could steal was a piece of lace or embroidery worth two to three cents. Leaving work we were treated worse than prisoners."

After the fire a member of the Women's Trade Union League consulted a fire expert as to what could be done about locked doors such as these, which are plenty enough in New York. Said he:

"Yes, the doors ought to be open, of course. It's all right to talk about it. But practically, you know—practically it can't be done! Why, if you had doors open so that the girls could come and go, they might get away with a lot of stuff. Why, the doors have got to be locked. Haven't you got to protect the manufacturer?"

And this not a week after the fire!

But there is still the question:

"Why didn't the girls come down the fire escape? There was one, wasn't there?"

Yes, there was one—just one! According to the official report, if there had been no fright or panic this fire escape would have emptied the building in three hours. The girls were all dead in twenty minutes!

Then again why did not the girls use the fire extinguishers apparatus required by law to be put in buildings of that class?

Said Mr. Harris of the firm on the witness stand:

"I can truthfully say that I never saw a length of hose or stand-pipe in the building."

An order had gone out to install automatic sprinklers in factories, but the manufacturers had organized to fight it because it meant so great an expenditure.

No! there seems to be no doubt of the reasons which prevented the girls from either using the fire escape or putting out the fire themselves.

Well, the fire is over, the girls are dead, and as I write the procession in honor of the unidentified dead is moving by under my windows. Now what is going to be done about it?

Harris and Blanck, the Triangle Company, have offered to pay one week's wages to the families of the dead girls—as though it were summer and they were giving them a vacation! Three days after the fire they inserted in the trade papers this notice:

"NOTICE, THE TRIANGLE WAIST CO. beg to notify their customers that they are in good working order. HEADQUARTERS now at 9–11 University Place."

The day after they were installed in their new quarters, the Building Department of New York City, discovered that 9-11 University Place, was not even fire proof and that the firm had already blocked the exit to the one fire escape by two rows of sewing machines, 75 in a row, and that at the same time repairs were begun on the old quarters in the burned building under a permit which called for no improvements or alterations of any conditions existing before the fire. It called for repairs only, which means, it was generally conceded, that the place would be re-opened in the same condition it was in before the fire.

That is what the employers have done.

The public has held meetings of protest—many of them. It has passed resolutions and subscribed over $80,000, to be expended through the Red Cross Society and a Citizens' Committee formed for the purpose.

What have the girls, working through their union, done for themselves? $15,000 was collected by the Ladies' Waist Makers' Union, the Forwards and the W. T. U. L. for the relief of the bereft families.

Early on the morning of the day after the fire, a meeting of the Executive Board of the Ladies' Waist and Dressmakers' Union was called, and relief work begun, no one knowing better than the girls who worked in the same trade what it meant to a family when the bread winner brought home no money on Saturday night. The girls themselves contributed, there was a call for funds throughout the unions and relief visitors were sent out within an hour. The Union offered to bury all unclaimed bodies and during the week following the fire the Relief Committee arranged for 21 burials. Not all of those buried were union members, as the Committee drew no line. Beside the burials immediate relief in the shape of cash payments and medical attendance has been given and rent falling due on the first of the month has been paid. The Union has four classes of cases to consider: First, where families were deprived of all support. Second, where the dependent families are in Europe. Third, where partial support of families has been lost. Fourth, where people were injured and have to be helped until they are well. A compensation act was declared unconstitutional a few days before this fire. The community lays the burden on the workers and safeguards the employers. The Executive Board of the Union has also instructed its attorneys to make such an investigation as will place the blame where it belongs with a view to criminal prosecution. . . .

Of course honorable gentlemen and influential boards have met together in great auditoriums and pled with the people. Said the Governor of the State:

"I want to assure you that my co-operation will be extended with a firm belief that a repetition of the Washington Square disaster will be avoided."

Said a great banker:

"The conditions which led to the Washington Place disaster should never again be allowed to exist in the city."

A professor from the University pled for a concentrated fire department so that we would know in future where to place the blame.

Said a Jewish Rabbi:

"We demand industrial peace with security for all."

But how are these things different from what we heard after [other disasters]? Have not the workers been begged before to preserve a judicial attitude? But you can't impose a judicial attitude on a mother two of whose children have been burned to death before her eyes. Neither can you on seven hundred and fifty thousand people who think their daughters may be burned to death tomorrow.

Said Peter Brady, of the Allied Printing Trades, in answer to the honorable gentlemen and the influential boards:

"We have very little confidence in your Citizens' Organization. Not so much as in Capitalistic Greed and Political Neglect."

And Rose Schneiderman of the Cloth Hat and Cap Makers' Union put it more definitely still when she said last Sunday in the Metropolitan Opera House:

"This is not the first time men and women have been burned to death. The life of men and women is so cheap, property is so sacred, there are so many of us to every job, that it matters little if 143 die. . . ."

And still as I write the mourning procession moves past in the rain. For two hours they have been going steadily by and the end is not yet in sight. There have been no carriages, no imposing marshals on horseback; just thousands on thousands of working men and women carrying the banners of their trades through the long three mile tramp in the rain. Never have I seen a military pageant or triumphant ovation so impressive; for it is not because one hundred and forty-three workers were killed in the Triangle Shop—not altogether. It is because every year there are fifty thousand working men and women killed in the United States—one hundred and thirty-six a day; almost as many as happened to be killed together on the 25th of March: and because slowly, very slowly, it is dawning on these thousands on thousands that such things do not have to be!

It is four hours later and the last of the procession has just passed.

4

"The Fire That Lit the Nation": Investigations and Reform

20

THE OUTLOOK

Indictments in the Asch Fire Case

April 22, 1911

At the grand jury hearing, District Attorney Whitman introduced the charred bolt from the locked door as evidence of the owners' guilt. But a locked door alone would result only in a misdemeanor and a small fine. A locked door, however, that resulted in the death of workers enabled Whitman to charge Blanck and Harris with manslaughter, which could mean up to twenty years in prison.

The magazine The Outlook *offered sympathetic coverage of the fire's victims and their families. Its coverage of garment strikes, however, suggested an editorial preference for arbitration to striking, including an endorsement of the Protocol of Peace established after the 1910 cloakmakers' strike.*

Last week the Grand Jury of New York found indictments against the proprietors of the Triangle Waist Company, Isaac Harris and Max Blanck. These two men constitute the firm who employed the factory operatives of whom 143 lost their lives in the terrible disaster in Washington Place, New York City, on March 25. The indictments against them are for manslaughter in the first and second degree, and

From "Indictments in the Asch Fire Case," *The Outlook*, April 22, 1911, 851.

they are based, so the District Attorney states, on what he believes to be strong evidence that some at least of the doors through which the girls might have escaped were habitually kept locked and were locked at the time of the fire. The law requires that doors in such a factory shall open outwardly where practicable, and shall not be locked, bolted, or fastened during working hours. The evidence before the coroner's jury has been conflicting on this point, but the Grand Jury, it is asserted, had before it a fragment of a tightly locked door. Meanwhile, Mr. Whitman, the District Attorney, laid before the Grand Jury the testimony of witnesses who stated that the doors on the Washington Place side of the building were kept locked, and the Italian Consul is reported to have taken the affidavits of many Italian girls who swore that the Washington Place doors were locked and never used for exit. It is further asserted that it is capable of proof that two girls in particular lost their lives directly because these doors were locked. We need not point out that the men accused are entitled to a suspension of opinion until they are actually tried. Whatever may be the facts in this case, there is considerable evidence that it is a deplorably common custom for doors in similar establishments to be locked. Immediately after the fire *The Outlook* quoted from the report of a special committee made up from the Cloakmakers' Union and the Cloak Manufacturers' Association. It stated that they had found twenty-two shops in which the doors leading to the hall and stairways were locked during the day, while other provisions of law were constantly violated in a much larger number of shops. The continuance of public interest in this matter and the wide discussion of proper legal regulation of conditions in factories and other crowded buildings in New York City form an encouraging sign that the public is in earnest and will not be satisfied with less than a thorough overhauling of the laws and the provision of an ample force of inspectors.

21

THE LITERARY DIGEST

147 Dead, Nobody Guilty

January 6, 1912

The furor over the dismissal of the case would not die down. "There was never a case," observed District Attorney Charles Whitman, "when the public demanded blood so strongly." In March 1912 thousands turned out for a memorial service for the victims and heard speeches in Italian, Yiddish, and English — all calling for a new trial. They denounced the judicial system as a glaring failure and repudiated the New York Times *for supporting the acquittal. Bowing to public pressure, Whitman filed new charges against Blanck and Harris, which were subsequently dismissed.*

Nine months ago 147 persons, chiefly young women and girls, were killed by a fire in the factory of the Triangle Waist Company at Washington Place and Greene Street, New York. All the subsequent evidence, as well as the facts of the tragedy, convinced the New York papers that this factory where hundreds of girls were compelled by circumstances to work for their livings was a veritable fire-trap, tho not worse, perhaps, than hundreds of other buildings in the city. Last week Isaac Harris and Max Blanck, owners of the Triangle Company, under trial for manslaughter in the first or second degree, were acquitted by a New York jury on their third ballot, after being out an hour and forty-five minutes. While the press in the main seem inclined to accept the verdict itself without serious challenge, many papers are gravely troubled over its practical implication that no one is responsible for that wholesale slaughter, and the feeling is widely exprest that, whatever the explanation of the outcome, justice has in fact been balked. It is "one of those disheartening failures of justice which are all too common in this country," declares the New York *Tribune*, which goes on to say:

> "Of all the various individuals who should have known that the hundreds of shirtwaist workers in Harris & Blanck's place worked in peril of their lives — proprietors of the factory, city and state

From "147 Dead, Nobody Guilty," *The Literary Digest*, January 6, 1912, 6.

inspectors, superintendents, and those who passed on plans and licenses, all the personnel engaged in the empty farce of protecting lives in workshops—out of the whole list of those whose responsibility seemed more or less obvious, the public prosecutor chose the proprietors as the ones whose responsibility might most surely be demonstrated. The charges against them have not been established to the satisfaction of a jury. There is little hope that the bringing home of personal guilt to any one of the many who took desperate chances with the lives of those workers in Washington Place may teach a salutary lesson of official or private responsibility.

"The monstrous conclusion of the law is that the slaughter was no one's fault, that it couldn't be helped, or perhaps even that, in the fine legal phrase which is big enough to cover a multitude of defects of justice, it was 'an act of God!' This conclusion is revolting to the moral sense of the community. . . .

"Is the fault with a system that makes all convictions difficult by excessive safeguards afforded to the accused? Does the law further fail in fixing a proper responsibility on owner and employers? If respect for law is to grow and not diminish, these defeats of justice, humiliating to society and repugnant to the individual conscience, must stop."

The point of view of those who must day after day submit themselves to risks similar to those which obtained in the Triangle factory is thus voiced by the New York *Call* (Socialist):

"There are no guilty. There are only the dead, and the authorities will forget the case as speedily as possible.

"Capital can commit no crime when it is in pursuit of profits.

"Of course, it is well known that those who were killed in the Triangle disaster are only part, and a small part, of those murdered in industry during the passing year. There were only 147 incinerated and mangled. But there were thousands of others who met a similarly agonizing fate during this year of 1911."

22

CHICAGO DAILY TRIBUNE

What the Grave Covers

September 30, 1913

The history of fires at the Triangle factory and the behavior of the owners, especially that of Max Blanck after the Triangle tragedy, heightened public anger and strengthened the belief that the owners were not only guilty but also callously indifferent to the law and their workers. Indeed, even after Blanck was fined $20 for locking a door to his new factory, several months later an investigator for the fire prevention bureau censured the Triangle Waist Company for continuing to violate workplace regulations.

Three years after the fire, in March 1914, Blanck and Harris agreed to settle twenty-three civil lawsuits filed by families of the victims. They paid $75 for each life lost. News of the paltry settlements stirred fresh controversy. Indeed, according to the first chronicler of the fire, Leon Stein, the Triangle owners collected enough fire insurance to make a profit of $445 on every worker killed.

In March, 1911, fire started in the factory of the Triangle Waist company in New York and 147 girls lost their lives. Fifty bodies, some of them burned to cinders, lying in a heap in front of a bolted door on the ninth floor of the factory, made clear the cause of the staggering loss of life. Escape had been cut off to these unfortunates by the locked door.

When the trial of the owners of the Triangle shop, Max Blanck and Isaac Harris, was called, the state produced in court a part of that ill fated door with the bolted lock in it. Evidence was heaped mountain high to prove that the girls in the Triangle shop were always locked in like cattle throughout the working day. Had the doors been open, witness after witness testified, most of the victims, if not all, might have saved themselves.

The record of Harris and Blanck was brought to light. It was found that they had had about half a dozen fires in their establishment on various occasions prior to the great holocaust, and that in each of

---

From "What the Grave Covers," *Chicago Daily Tribune*, September 30, 1913, p. 6.

these fires the workers had a narrow escape from death. The trial lasted five weeks. The judge's charge to the jury lasted an hour. In that charge the judge, singularly enough, had nothing to say about the bolted lock, which really fixed the blame for the death of 147 persons. Harris and Blanck went free.

The other day Max Blanck was again arrested. He was found guilty of having the doors of his factory locked, as they were locked on the day of each fire. Justice was meted out to him. He was fined $20.

When Harris and Blanck were acquitted of the manslaughter charge at the first trial the alien parents and friends of 147 victims of the Triangle fire wept hysterically and declared that there is no justice for poor people in America, and that the law is here solely to protect the rich and oppress the poor. If this unbelievable report is true, what must they, what must we think?

There is a saying, "what the grave covers is speedily forgotten." But the 147 victims of the Triangle fire, now earth covered, should not be forgotten. They should serve as a reminder that, in spite of all recent crusades for safety in factories, there are still scores of thousands of girls in New York and elsewhere whose lives might be snuffed out any moment by locked factory doors. A heavy fine and a prison term for Max Blanck would have served as a warning to others of his kind that they cannot endanger lives of employes with impunity. The fine of $20 only strengthens Max Blanck and manufacturers of his type in the view they now hold, and which many of them privately express not only in actions but in words also, that the workers they employ are merely "rats," whose life or death nobody, no court or jury, takes very seriously.

23

STATE OF NEW YORK

Preliminary Report of the Factory Investigating Commission
1912

Although Mary Dreier of the WTUL was the lone woman on the FIC, the investigative process drew on the talents of many women reformers who had been active in labor organizations, the Consumers' League, and many other associations. The FIC enhanced the political visibility of women and recruited new women to the Democratic party. Clara Lemlich, Rose Schneiderman, Pauline Newman, and Frances Perkins all played important roles in the investigations. Thanks to their determined commitment to women workers, they ensured that the male members of the commission visited women's workplaces, from garment factories to canneries, and that they heard the testimony of women workers themselves.

Women who testified proved very willing to detail their work conditions and wages but were more reluctant to discuss their private circumstances, offering fewer details about their families. Counseled by their parents that such information was confidential and fearful that something might be somehow used against them, they were often circumspect in responding to personal questions.

ROSE FERRIGNO, called as a witness, not sworn, testified as follows:

By Mr. ELKUS:

Q. What is your name? A. Rose Ferrigno.
Q. How old are you? A. Fifteen; I am going on sixteen.
Q. Were you born in this city of New York? A. Yes, sir.
Q. Where do you live? A. 24 Monroe.
Q. What is your father's name? A. Salvatore Ferrigno.
Q. What does your father do? A. He does not work.
Q. What is the matter with him? A. He was sick.

From State of New York, *Preliminary Report of the Factory Investigating Commission, 1912*, Volume III (Albany, N.Y.: The Argus Company, 1912), 1782–84.

Q. Is he sick now? A. He is a little better now.

Q. How long has he been sick? A. About four years.

Q. Been in the hospital? A. No.

Q. Sick at home? A. Yes, sir.

Q. How many brothers and sisters have you? A. One brother and four sisters.

Q. Are they younger or older than you? A. Younger.

Q. How old is the younger? A. Two years.

Q. You are the oldest? A. I am the oldest.

Q. None of them work besides you? A. No, sir.

Q. Does your mother work? A. Yes, sir.

Q. What does she do? A. She works at home.

Q. What kind of work does she do? A. Coats.

Q. Sews on coats? A. Yes, sir.

Q. Men's clothes? A. Pants, yes.

Q. Do your sisters help or do your brothers? A. No; they are too small.

Q. They are all too small? A. Yes, sir.

Q. They go to school? A. Yes, sir.

Q. Except the two-year-old one? A. Yes, sir.

Q. Where do you work now? A. Shay Bros., shirtwaists.

Q. Where are they located, where is the place of business? A. 546 and 548 Broadway.

Q. The same place as the last little girl? A. Yes, sir.

Q. Are you a girl that keeps count of spools? A. Floor girl, yes, sir.

Q. How long have you been working there? A. About seven or eight months.

Q. How much do you get a week? A. Five dollars.

Q. You do the same as she does and you get five dollars a week? A. Yes, sir.

Q. What time do you get there in the morning? A. Eight.

Q. What time do you leave at night? A. Five.

Q. An hour you have for lunch? A. Yes, sir.

Q. Do you walk from your home there every morning? A. Yes, sir.

Q. And back at night? A. Yes, sir.

Q. And do you walk up and down all the time while you are there except when you are at lunch? A. Yes, sir.

Q. Where do you eat your lunch? A. Right there in the place.

Q. Do you sit down when you eat your lunch? A. Yes, sir.

Q. You bring your lunch with you, I suppose? A. Yes, sir.

Q. And do you feel tired? A. No, sir.

Q. Never feel tired? A. No, sir.

Q. Do you go to school here? A. I used to go to school.

Q. What class were you in? A. Five B, after I got my working papers.

Q. Then you had three years more to go before you graduated. Why didn't you go through school? A. I couldn't go.

Q. What? A. Didn't want to go.

Q. What is the matter with your father? A. He was sick.

Q. What is the matter with him? A. Couldn't work.

Q. What is the trouble with him? A. I don't know.

Q. Don't you know; has he got a cold? A. No; he used to go to the hospital; they wanted to keep him in the hospital.

Q. Wouldn't he stay? A. Yes, wanted to stay; he didn't want to go no more.

Q. How old is your father? A. About forty-seven.

By Commissioner GOMPERS:

Q. You say your mother does sewing on pants? A. Yes, sir.

Q. You have four brothers and one sister? A. Four sisters and one brother.

Q. Do you help your mother in her work sometimes? A. No, sir.

Q. Any of your brothers or any of your sisters help her? A. No, sir.

Q. Don't do anything? A. No, sir.

Q. Picking out bastings? A. Sometimes they do that when they come from school at three o'clock.

Q. They help her, then, in that way? A. Yes, sir.

Q. In no other way? A. No, sir.

By Commissioner DREIER:

Q. How much money does your mother make a week? A. Sometimes five dollars, sometimes six dollars a week.

Q. Then you and your mother support the family? A. Yes, sir.

Q. That is all the money you get? A. Yes, sir.

By Commissioner GOMPERS:

Q. How old is your father? A. Forty-seven.

Mr. ELKUS: There are several other children here, but they are all the same, and I won't call them unless you desire it. It is simply to give you an idea of what is going on right here in the city.

24

ALFRED E. SMITH

Up to Now: An Autobiography
1929

Al Smith and FIC chair Robert Wagner, known as the "Tammany Twins," took the legislature by storm, pushing through reform bills by the dozens as they adopted the Progressive reform language of social justice, state responsibility, and industrial morality. They were formidable fighters, silencing opposition and securing broader change than anyone anticipated. By the end of 1913, they had remedied most of the safety problems that had plagued the Triangle factory, requiring sprinklers in loft factories, fire drills, and unlocked doors that opened out.

Called the "happy warrior," Smith went on to become the Democratic nominee for the presidency in 1928.

The whole state of New York was shocked by the terrible catastrophe caused by a fire occurring on March 25, 1911, in the factory of the Triangle Waist Company, in which 148 employees, chiefly women and girls, lost their lives. There was an immediate conviction in the public mind that this appalling disaster resulted from neglect to enforce laws for the protection of the lives of people in factory buildings.

The fire started from a cigarette thrown among some waste material. Obstructed avenues of exit and a locked door were the direct causes of the great loss of life. The building itself was fireproof, and nothing burned but the contents of the rooms devoted to the making of shirtwaists, but the locked door and blocking of the aisles of exit caused this enormous loss of life in a very few minutes. The newspapers of the time contained the shocking details of women and girls jumping from the windows only to be crushed to death on the pavement.

A Committee on Safety was immediately formed to meet the public protest. . . . The Committee immediately called a mass meeting in the Metropolitan Opera House and a resolution was offered by Henry

---

From Alfred E. Smith, *Up to Now: An Autobiography* (New York: The Viking Press, 1929), 90–98.

Moskowitz, then head worker in an East Side Settlement, calling on the legislature to make a thorough investigation of safety conditions in factories and to pass laws to prevent a recurrence of such a catastrophe. . . .

They sought me out and asked for help in the formulation of remedies to prevent future disasters. Conferences with them and with Senator Wagner, then leader of the state senate, developed the necessity of a thorough study. A commission was suggested. The bill to create it was introduced into the senate by Senator Wagner and into the assembly by myself. It was practically unopposed, although later there was severe opposition manifested in both houses to a great many of the measures recommended by it.

The commission was composed of two members of the senate, three members of the assembly, and four citizens appointed by the governor. Senator Robert F. Wagner was elected chairman and I was the vice chairman. . . .

So lax had the state been prior to 1911, that the commission hardly began its labors when it was discovered that there was no way for the state even to know when a factory was started. A man could hire a floor in a loft building, put in his machinery, and start his factory. There was no provision of law that required him to notify the state that he was engaging in a business which came under the supervision of a department of the state government.

Factory-inspection forces were so small that the inspections in some cities were made only once in two years and in others once a year. Factory managers knew just about when to expect an inspection, and consequently, during the day of the inspector's visit everything was in ship shape. The rest of the year it was allowed to run haphazard, there being no fear of detection by the authorities in charge of the Department of Labor. Once an inspector arrived at a factory a day ahead of time. There were children under the legal age employed in that particular factory and these were hastily put into the elevators, the cars were run between the floors and kept there until the inspector left. . . .

It was during the course of the investigations made by this commission that I got my first good look at the state of New York. The commission met in practically every city in the state. I afterward derived much benefit from the personal inspections we had made, because, as leader of the Democrats in the assembly, it was up to me to lead the battle for the enactment of these statutes in the lower house. . . .

We have always had, in both houses of the legislature, senators and assemblymen who represent counties in the state which have no factories in them, and they opposed many of these laws. In fact, after the close of the Factory Commission's work, a manufacturers' association was organized which maintained a paid representative at Albany, and still does, to oppose the enactment of laws regulating and prescribing conditions of labor.

In the first year of its existence the commission proposed and passed laws controlling the sanitary conditions of factories, regulating the labor of women and children, and providing fire-prevention measures and regular fire drills. One of the important statutes resulting from our investigation was the prohibition of night work for women in factory buildings. . . .

It was interesting to me to see how the reactionary legislator who was unfriendly to this kind of legislation would always manage to find such strong legal and constitutional arguments against it. Always declaring in favor of the principle and being in complete harmony and sympathy with what was sought to be done, the clever debater could invariably find a way of explaining that, in his opinion, the proposed enactment would not bring about the result desired. Although he himself had no suggestion to cure the wrong that was so apparent from the studies of the investigating commission, he could always find such legislation was either in opposition to the constitution or improperly drawn.

25

FRANCES PERKINS

The Roosevelt I Knew

1946

Middle-class reformer and eyewitness to the Triangle fire, Frances Perkins impressed reformers and political leaders alike in her role as an investigator for the FIC. She not only befriended Al Smith and Robert Wagner but became dearest of friends with trade unionists Rose Schneiderman and Pauline Newman. As governor of New York in 1928, Franklin D. Roosevelt named Perkins as the first woman industrial commissioner in

From Frances Perkins, *The Roosevelt I Knew* (New York: The Viking Press, 1946), 17, 22–23.

the nation, and later, as president, he appointed her as the first woman secretary of labor. At the state and national level, Perkins remained loyal to the women and the issues of the WTUL.

Alfred E. Smith and Robert Wagner, who later became great leaders in the state and nation in social justice achieved by legislative techniques, got their education as members of the Factory Investigation Commission appointed by the state legislature after the terrible Triangle Factory fire in New York City, March 25, 1911. They got a firsthand look at industrial and labor conditions, and from that look they never recovered. They became firm and unshakable sponsors of political and legislative measures designed to overcome conditions unfavorable to human life. . . .

I was an investigator for the Factory Investigation Commission and we used to make it our business to take Al Smith, the East Side boy who later became New York's Governor and a presidential candidate, to see the women, thousands of them, coming off the ten-hour nightshift on the rope walks in Auburn. . . . We saw to it that the austere legislative members of the Commission got up at dawn and drove with us for an unannounced visit to a Cattaraugus County cannery and that they saw with their own eyes the little children, not adolescents, but five-, six-, and seven-year-olds, snipping beans and shelling peas. We made sure that they saw the machinery that would scalp a girl or cut off a man's arm. Hours so long that both men and women were depleted and exhausted became realities to them through seeing for themselves the dirty little factories. These men realized something could be done about it from discussions with New York State employers who had succeeded in remedying adverse working conditions and standards of pay. Such a man was Edmund Huyck, a blanket and wool textile manufacturer at Rensselaer; such businesses were the Carolyn Laundry in the Bronx and a concern in Rochester with the strange name of "Art in Buttons."

It was the experiments of these and other manufacturers (all successful moneymakers) that brought conviction to the members of the Commission that conditions in industry were frequently bad for the workers; that they were correctable by practical means; and that correction by lawful process would benefit industries as well as workers. Production and business would increase and the whole state would profit.

These principles the Commission recommended, and the legislature, over a period of three to five years, put into law the program of compulsory shorter work day and week for women, limitation of age of children at work, prohibition of night work for women, workmen's compensation for industrial accidents, measures to prevent industrial accidents, and elaborate requirements for the construction of factory and mercantile premises in the interests of the health and safety of the people who worked in them.

The extent to which this legislation in New York marked a change in American political attitudes and policies toward social responsibility can scarcely be overrated. It was, I am convinced, a turning point; it was not only successful in effecting practical remedies but, surprisingly, it proved to be successful also in vote-getting.

A Chronology of the Triangle Fire
(1900–2001)

1900 The International Ladies Garment Workers Union (ILGWU) is formed.

1901 Construction of the ten-story fireproof Asch loft building is completed.

1902 Max Blanck and Isaac Harris open the Triangle Waist Company on the ninth floor of the Asch Building.

1903 A small group of women reformers and settlement house workers join together to form the Women's Trade Union League (WTUL) of New York.

1909 The Triangle factory now occupies the eighth, ninth, and tenth floors of the Asch Building, and Blanck and Harris become known as the "Shirtwaist Kings." They increase insurance coverage of their company but ignore recommendations for fire drills.

ILGWU's Local 25 announces a strike against the Triangle factory.

November 22: Clara Lemlich of the ILGWU gives an electrifying speech, calling for a general strike. The next morning, on November 23, the "great uprising" begins.

Blanck and Harris unsuccessfully attempt to break the strike.

December: After the arrests of hundreds of strikers, the ILGWU and the WTUL organize a mass meeting and march on City Hall to protest police treatment of strikers.

1910 *February*: After more than three hundred firms recognize the union, the ILGWU declares the strike officially over. The Triangle Waist Company, however, refuses to grant union recognition.

July: The "great revolt" of the cloakmakers begins.

September: The great revolt ends with the adoption of the Protocol of Peace—a type of industrial self-government that brings together leaders from labor, business, and the public.

1911 *March 25*: At about 4:45 p.m., fire breaks out on the eighth floor and quickly spreads to the ninth and tenth floors. Workers begin leaping from the burning building. Fire trucks arrive within minutes, but neither the water hoses nor the ladders can reach the upper floors of the factory. The fire is contained within thirty minutes, but firefighters continue to remove bodies from the building until nearly midnight. Corpses are loaded onto wagons and transferred to a pier hastily transformed into a temporary morgue.

March 26: Over a hundred thousand people stream into the morgue to examine the bodies. The Red Cross and the ILGWU, assisted by the WTUL, begin campaigns to assist survivors and families of victims.

April 2: Thousands of workers and sympathizers turn out at the Metropolitan Opera House to protest the calamity and call for reform. Rose Schneiderman ignites the audience with a stirring speech.

April 5: A massive funeral procession organized by the ILGWU threads through the streets of the city to pay respects to the seven unidentified bodies. Officials place the total number of deaths at 146.

April 11: Triangle owners Isaac Harris and Max Blanck are indicted for manslaughter, but the trial is postponed until December.

June 30: Governor John Dix signs legislation creating the Factory Investigating Commission (FIC).

December: The trial of Harris and Blanck begins, drawing anger from the community. Contingents of police are dispatched to control the crowd and protect the defendants.

December 27: After fewer than two hours of deliberation, the jury finds Blanck and Harris not guilty.

1912 *February*: The WTUL, women workers, and families of victims organize a massive rally denouncing the acquittal of Blanck and Harris and demanding additional charges. The district attorney issues new indictments, but the case is dismissed in March.

March 25: A memorial service is held to remember the Triangle victims; women garment workers in the city and the nation stop work and stand in silence to honor their sister workers, beginning a tradition that continues for years.

1913 The FIC presents dozens of factory reforms, which are passed by the legislature and signed into law by the governor. Other states begin examining factory safety.

September: Max Blanck is fined $20 for locking a door at a new shirtwaist factory.

1914   Blanck and Harris agree to settle civil suits filed by relatives of the victims, paying $75 for each life lost.

To pay tribute to the victims and to acknowledge the fire's impetus for major reform, the third anniversary of the Triangle tragedy is observed by the ringing of bells 146 times, the cessation of work for several minutes of quiet observance, and the holding of newly required fire drills in factories throughout the city.

1918   The Triangle Waist Company ceases to exist.

1961   On the fiftieth anniversary of the fire, Eleanor Roosevelt, former secretary of labor Frances Perkins, and labor activist Rose Schneiderman, along with several Triangle survivors, join ILGWU leaders in placing a plaque on the corner of the Asch Building in honor of the Triangle workers.

1991   The National Park Service officially designates the Asch Building (now renamed the Brown Building and owned by New York University) a national historic landmark in recognition of the Triangle victims.

2001   Rose Freedman, the last survivor of the Triangle fire, dies at age 107 after devoting her life to promoting industrial reform and worker safety.

Questions for Consideration

1. Why did manufacturers of shirtwaists use loft factories? What were the economic advantages? What were the safety hazards?

2. The growth of the shirtwaist industry jumped significantly in the first decade of the twentieth century. Who provided the labor supply for the production of shirtwaists? What kind of training did the workers receive? How did the industry's seasonality affect these workers and their wages?

3. Why did Progressive reformers target the garment industry for their reform efforts? What kinds of reform did they seek to achieve?

4. How would you describe the workday of immigrant women who made shirtwaists? What did they like about their experiences as women workers? What did they dislike?

5. What provoked the great uprising of 1909? What were the objectives of the strikers? What were the roles of the Women's Trade Union League and the International Ladies Garment Workers Union?

6. The general strike stirred both sympathy and animosity. How did gender, class, and ethnicity affect the strike and the strikers? Describe the complex ways in which the city responded to this unprecedented upheaval.

7. What were the outcomes of the strike? Was it a success or a failure? What happened at the Triangle factory?

8. What was the reaction to the Triangle fire in the city, the state, and the nation? Why did many observers link the fire with the earlier strike against the Triangle factory? How did the ILGWU and the WTUL respond to the tragedy? How did workers respond?

9. The Triangle fire raised critical questions about the regulatory role of government in society, especially pointing to the issues of worker safety and management rights. What were these questions, and how did workers, reformers, and civic and business leaders respond to them?

10. What was the impact of the fire on state and local politics? How did the Tammany Hall political machine respond? What was the mission of the Factory Investigating Commission (FIC)? What did it find in its investigations?

11. In the excerpt from his autobiography, Alfred Smith praises the law prohibiting night work for women as one of the most important statutes passed. How might such a law also work against the interests of women workers?

12. The Triangle fire produced immediate and significant change. Assess the consequences of the fire for the Progressive Era, especially the impact on women and factory work. Why do you think the Triangle fire has been called the "fire that changed America"?

Selected Bibliography

IMMIGRATION, REFORM, AND THE PROGRESSIVE ERA

Boyer, Paul. *Urban Masses and Moral Order in America, 1820–1920*. Cambridge, Mass.: Harvard University Press, 1978.

Buenker, John D. *Urban Liberalism and Progressive Reform*. New York: W. W. Norton, 1978.

Connolly, James J. *The Triumph of Ethnic Progressivism: Urban Political Culture in Boston*. Cambridge, Mass.: Harvard University Press, 1998.

Diner, Hasia R., Jeffrey Sandler, and Beth S. Wenger, eds. *Remembering the Lower East Side: American Jewish Reflections*. Bloomington: Indiana University Press, 2000.

DuBois, Ellen Carol. *Harriot Stanton Blatch and the Winning of Woman Suffrage*. New Haven, Conn.: Yale University Press, 1997.

Flanagan, Maureen A. *Seeing With Their Hearts: Chicago Women and the Vision of the Good City, 1871–1933*. Princeton, N.J.: Princeton University Press, 2002.

Henderson, Thomas M. *Tammany Hall and the New Immigrants: The Progressive Years*. New York: Arno Books, 1976.

Howe, Irving. *World of Our Fathers: The Journey of the Eastern European Jews to America and the Life They Found and Made*. New York: Touchstone (Simon & Schuster), 1976.

Huthmacher, J. Joseph. *Senator Robert F. Wagner and the Rise of Urban Liberalism*. New York: Atheneum, 1968.

Lehrer, Susan. *Origins of Protective Labor Legislation for Women, 1905–1925*. Albany: State University of New York Press, 1987.

Morrison, Joan, and Charlotte Fox Zabusky, eds. *American Mosaic: The Immigrant Experience in the Words of Those Who Lived It*. New York: E. P. Dutton, 1980.

Muncy, Robyn. *Creating a Female Dominion in American Reform, 1890–1935*. New York: Oxford University Press, 1991.

Perry, Elisabeth Israels. *Belle Moskowitz: Feminine Politics and the Exercise of Power in the Age of Alfred E. Smith*. New York: Oxford University Press, 1987.

Rodgers, Daniel T. *Atlantic Crossings: Social Politics in a Progressive Age*. Cambridge, Mass.: Harvard University Press, 1998.

Weinberg, Sydney Stahl. *The World of Our Mothers: The Lives of Jewish Immigrant Women*. Chapel Hill: University of North Carolina Press, 1988.

Weiss, Nancy Joan. *Charles Francis Murphy, 1858–1924: Respectability and Responsibility in Tammany Politics*. Northampton, Mass.: Smith College, 1968.

WOMEN, WORK, AND THE GARMENT INDUSTRY

Argersinger, Jo Ann E. *Making the Amalgamated: Gender, Ethnicity, and Class in the Baltimore Clothing Industry, 1899–1939*. Baltimore: Johns Hopkins University Press, 1999.

Buhle, Mari Jo. *Women and American Socialism, 1870–1920*. Urbana: University of Illinois Press, 1983.

Dye, Nancy Schrom. *As Equals and As Sisters: Feminism, the Labor Movement, and the Women's Trade Union League of New York*. Columbia: University of Missouri Press, 1980.

Eisenstein, Sarah. *Give Us Bread But Give Us Roses: Working Women's Consciousness in the United States, 1890 to the First World War*. London and Boston: Routledge and Kegan Paul, 1983.

Enstad, Nan. *Ladies of Labor, Girls of Adventure: Working Women, Popular Culture, and Labor Politics at the Turn of the Twentieth Century*. New York: Columbia University Press, 1999.

Ewen, Elizabeth. *Immigrant Women in the Land of Dollars: Life and Culture on the Lower East Side, 1890–1925*. New York: Monthly Review Press, 1985.

Friedman-Kasaba, Kathie. *Memories of Migration: Gender, Ethnicity, and Work in the Lives of Jewish and Italian Women in New York, 1870–1924*. Albany: State University of New York Press, 1996.

Glenn, Susan A. *Daughters of the Shtetl: Life and Labor in the Immigrant Generation*. Ithaca, N.Y.: Cornell University Press, 1990.

Henry, Alice. *The Trade Union Woman*. New York: Burt Franklin, 1973.

Jensen, Joan M., and Sue Davidson, eds. *A Needle, A Bobbin, A Strike: Women Needleworkers in America*. Philadelphia: Temple University Press, 1984.

Kessler-Harris, Alice. *Out to Work: A History of Wage-Earning Women in the United States*. New York: Oxford University Press, 1983.

Levine, Louis. *The Women's Garment Workers: A History of the International Ladies' Garment Workers' Union*. New York: B. W. Huebsch, 1924.

McCreesh, Carolyn D. *Women in the Campaign to Organize Garment Workers, 1880–1917*. New York: Garland, 1985.

Milbank, Caroline Rennolds. *New York Fashion: The Evolution of American Style*. New York: Harry N. Abrams, 1989.

Miller, Sally, ed. *Race, Ethnicity, and Gender in Early Twentieth-Century American Socialism*. New York: Garland, 1996.

Murolo, Priscilla. *The Common Ground of Womanhood: Class, Gender, and Working Girls' Clubs, 1884–1928*. Urbana: University of Illinois Press, 1997.

Orleck, Annelise. *Common Sense and a Little Fire: Women and Working-Class Politics in the United States, 1900–1965*. Chapel Hill: University of North Carolina Press, 1995.

Peiss, Kathy. *Cheap Amusements: Working Women and Leisure in Turn-of-the-Century New York*. Philadelphia: Temple University Press, 1986.

Schneiderman, Rose, with Lucy Goldthwaite. *All For One*. New York: Paul S. Eriksson, 1967.

Stein, Leon, ed. *Out of the Sweatshop: The Struggle for Industrial Democracy*. New York: Quadrangle, 1977.

Tax, Meredith. *The Rising of the Women: Feminist Solidarity and Class Conflict, 1880–1917*. New York: Monthly Review Press, 1980.

Waldinger, Roger D. "Another Look at the International Ladies' Garment Workers' Union: Women, Industry Structure, and Collective Action," in *Women, Work, and Protest: A Century of U.S. Women's Labor History*, ed. Ruth Milkman. Boston: Routledge and Kegan Paul, 1985, 86–95.

———. *Through the Eye of the Needle: Immigrants and Enterprise in New York's Garment Trades*. New York: New York University Press, 1986.

THE TRIANGLE FIRE AND ITS CONSEQUENCES

Behrens, Eric G. "The Triangle Shirtwaist Company Fire of 1911: A Lesson in Legislative Manipulation," *Texas Law Review* 62 (October 1983): 3–12.

Burns, Ric, and James Sanders. *New York: An Illustrated History*. New York: Alfred A. Knopf, 1999.

Greenwald, Richard A. *The Triangle Fire, the Protocols of Peace, and Industrial Democracy in Progressive Era New York*. Philadelphia: Temple University Press, 2005.

Jensen, Frances Brewer. "The Triangle Fire and the Limits of Progressivism." Ph.D. Dissertation, University of Massachusetts, Amherst, 1996.

Llewellyn, Chris. *Fragments from the Fire: The Triangle Shirtwaist Fire of March 25, 1911: Poems*. New York: Viking Penguin Books, 1987.

McClymer, John F. *The Triangle Strike and Fire*. Orlando, Fla.: Harcourt Brace College Publishers, 1998.

Perkins, Frances. *The Roosevelt I Knew*. New York: The Viking Press, 1946.

Severn, Bill. *Frances Perkins: A Member of the Cabinet*. New York: Hawthorn Books, 1976.

Stein, Leon. *The Triangle Fire*. Introduction by William Greider. Ithaca, N.Y.: Cornell University Press, 2001.

Von Drehle, David. *Triangle: The Fire That Changed America*. New York: Grove Press, 2003.

Waisala, Wendy Ellen. "To Bring Forth a Note of One's Own: Contested Memory and the Labor Literature of the Haymarket Tragedy, the Triangle Fire, and Joe Hill." Ph.D. Dissertation, New York University, 1997.

RELEVANT WEB SITES

"The Triangle Factory Fire" of Cornell University's Kheel Center for Labor-Management Documentation and Archives is the most comprehensive site dedicated to the study of the fire and its consequences. It features primary documents, photographs, and audio segments, including the complete transcript of the trial of Max Blanck and Isaac Harris. It also contains useful information and photographs on the "great uprising" of 1909. www.ilr.cornell.edu/trianglefire.

"Heaven Will Protect the Working Girl: Immigrant Women in the Turn-of-the Century City," a companion site to a video that focuses on the shirtwaist strike, offers a variety of resources, including primary documents and a bibliography for further research. The site is part of the American Social History Project and Center for Media and Learning at the City University of New York. www.ashp.cuny.edu/heaven/index.html.

"Women Working, 1800–1930" provides useful primary documents, especially relevant magazine articles. The collection contains a half million digitized pages and images. http://ocp.hul.harvard.edu/ww/.

"Women and Social Movements in the United States, 1600–2000" provides a number of important primary documents on the shirtwaist strike, conditions of work for women, and the efforts of reformers and labor organizations. The site is restricted to paid subscribers. http://womhist .alexanderstreet.com.

"Famous Trials" is a valuable resource for learning more about the trial of the Triangle owners. In addition to primary documents and images, the site provides a list of the victims by name. www.law.umkc.edu/faculty/ projects/ftrials/triangle/trianglefire.html.

Index

Addams, Jane, 10
aisles, blocked, 32
"All for One" (Schneiderman), 99–101
ambulances, 72, 78
American, 24
American Book Company Building, 81, 82
American Federationist, 69
American Federation of Labor (AFL), 32, 69
arrests, labor unions and, 16, 58–61, 67–68
"Arrest Strikers for Being Assaulted" (*New York Times*), 58–61
Asch, Joseph, 5
Asch Building, 2, 5. *See also* Triangle Waist Company
  city codes and, 26
  commemoration plaque, 33
  construction of, 5, 122
  designated national historic landmark, 124
  fire escapes, 41
  persons employed in, 73
Associated Waist and Dress Manufacturers, 43

Belmont, Alva (Mrs. O. H. P.), 65, 66, 68
Benani, Sarah, 104
Benani, Tessa, 104
Benson, Allan J.
  "Women in a Labor War: How the Working Girls of New York East Side Have Learned to Use Men's Weapons in a Struggle for Better Conditions," 61–65
Bergida, Sadie, 103
Blackwell's Island, 15, 68
Blanck, Henrietta, 79–80
Blanck, Max. *See also* Harris, Isaac
  account of fire by, 79–84, 105
  acquittal of, 29–30, 110–11, 113
  additional charges against, 30
  antiunion position, 12
  arrest of, 113
  bail paid by, 28
  business practices, 2, 4–5, 6
  children of, 79–81
  children's governess, 79–81
  chronology, 122–24
  civil rights suit, 30

evidence against, 27–28
family of, 17
fined for locking door at new factory, 30, 113
fire experiences, 79–80
on fire origins, 82–83
indictment of, 85, 108–9
indifference of, 27
insurance money collected by, 30
insurance on Triangle Waist Company, 39
lawsuits against, 112–13
new shirtwaist factory, 27
photograph, 7f
public demand for punishment of, 27–28, 112–13
response to strike by, 16, 59
roof escape, 17, 80–81, 104
supervision by, 11
trial of, 28–29
wealth of, 5
Blanck, Mildred, 79–80
blocked exits, 27, 32
blouses, 2. *See also* shirtwaists
bossism, 3
Brooklyn Bureau of Charities, 92
Brown, William, 104
Brown Building, 124
Bruere, Martha Bensley
  "Triangle Fire, The," 101–7
"Budgets of the Triangle Fire Victims" (Dutcher), 94–98
Building Department, New York City, 26, 84, 105
building inspections, 27, 82, 84, 105–6, 117–19
Butts, Magistrate, 68

Charity Organization Society, 92, 93
Chicago Daily Tribune
  "What the Grave Covers," 112–13
Chicago Sunday Tribune
  "Thrilling Incidents in Gotham Holocaust That Wiped Out One Hundred and Fifty Lives," 76–79
child labor, 49, 121
  at Triangle Waist Company, 6
  working conditions, 2

"Church to the Aid of Girl Workers" (*New York Times*), 66–68
Citizens' Committee, 106
city codes, 26
civil rights suits, 30
cloakmakers' union, 30, 71, 98, 109
  strike, 108
Cloak Manufacturers' Association, 109
Cloth Hat and Cap Makers' Union, 107
clothing
  fashion trends, 9–10
  of immigrant women workers, 55
  social class and, 10
coffins, 22f, 75, 78–79
Cohen, Rose, 46
  "Out of the Shadow," 46–50
commercialism, 9
Committee on Safety, 30, 117–18
Coney Island, 9, 54, 55
Consumers' League, 32, 114
contracting system, 44, 97
  garment industry, 6
  Triangle Waist Company, 11
Cooper Union, 62, 64
Cornell, Magistrate, 97
Costello, Della, 22
Croker, Fire Chief, 41, 73, 78
Cypress Hills Cemetery, 89, 90

dance halls, 9
De Cantillon, Joseph, 58–59
defense witnesses, 29
Democratic party, 3, 32–33. *See also* Tammany Hall
Deutchman, Ida, 104
dime novels, 9
Dix, John, 26, 31, 123
doors
  locked, 17, 18, 28, 29, 30, 32, 83, 85, 103–5, 108–9, 112–13, 117, 124
  narrow, 42
Dreier, Margaret. *See* Robins, Margaret Dreier
Dreier, Mary, 12, 15, 66, 68, 88, 114, 116
  arrest of, 58–61
Dutcher, Elizabeth
  "Budgets of the Triangle Fire Victims," 94–98

Eastern European Jews. *See* Jewish immigrant workers
education, 54–55
electric knives, 42
elevators
  escape using, 18, 73, 78, 81, 104
  freight, 83, 104
  in loft buildings, 42
  operators, 80
  tenth-floor workers' use of, 17, 83

Elkus, Mr., 114–16
"Emergency Relief after the Washington Place Fire: New York, March 25, 1911," 90–93
employers
  appeal of women workers to, 97
  investigations of, 119–21
  liability of, 33
  police support of, 59
  Tammany Hall protection of, 3
exits, blocked, 27, 32

factories. *See also* shirtwaist factories
  factory district, 40
  high-rise, 39–42
  immigrant women employees, 1, 2
  industrial accidents, 2
  investigations, 31
  "sweating," 2, 5
Factory Investigating Commission (FIC), 31–32, 99, 117–19, 120, 123
  preliminary report, 114–16
families, women workers and, 10, 25, 95–98
fashion trends, 6, 9–10
feller hands, 47–50
Ferrigno, Rose, 114–18
Ferrigno, Salvatore, 114
fines
  for strikers, 15, 97
  for workers, 8, 9, 11
fire alarm boxes, 83
"Fire and the Skyscraper: The Problem of Protecting Workers in New York's Tower Factories" (McFarlane), 39–42
fire buckets, 83
fire department
  loft buildings and, 41
  Triangle Waist Company fire, 1, 17–21, 19f, 21f
fire drills, 32, 122, 124
fire escapes
  Asch Building, 18, 20, 27, 32, 41, 73–74, 83, 86, 105
  collapse of, 18, 20
  loft buildings, 41
fire extinguishers, 105
fire hoses, 19f, 20, 27
fire ladders, 1, 103
fire nets, 1, 18, 103
fireproof buildings, 27, 74
flammable materials
  in shirtwaist factories, 42, 74
  in Triangle Waist Company, 42, 82
Freedman, Rose, 124
freight elevators, 83, 104
Froelich, Dr. Ralph A., 79
Frowne, Sadie
  "Story of a Sweatshop Girl, The," 50–55
funeral procession, for unidentifiable fire victims, 87–90, 101, 123

garment industry, 4–11. *See also* immigrant
    women workers; shirtwaist factories;
    Triangle Waist Company; women
    workers
  bosses, 57
  contracting system, 6
  factories, 6
  Italian immigrants and, 8
  Jewish immigrants and, 8
  labor unions and, 6, 12–13
  locations above seventh floor, 27
  in loft buildings, 40–41
  mass production in, 5
  piece work in, 8, 49, 56
  profits in, 6
  reform movements and, 3, 11, 14
  Sabbath and, 8, 52
  strikes, 15–16, 55, 56
  wages in, 8, 55, 56, 57
  women workers in, 6, 8–9
  working conditions, 9
  working hours, 55
gas irons, 42
gas lighting, 42
Gaynor, William, 25, 26, 87
Glantz, Rose, 17
Goldstein, Mary, 20
Goldstein, Yetta, 22*f*, 23
Gompers, Samuel L., 12, 32, 116
Goodman, Pearl, 43
Goodman, Pearl, and Elsa Ueland
    "Shirtwaist Trade, The," 43–46
"Gotham," 76
Grand Jury of New York, 108–9
Grasso, Rosie, 28
Great Hall, Cooper Union, meeting, 12–13
group (partnership) system, 44

Harris, Esther, 81–82
Harris, Isaac. *See also* Blanck, Max
  account of fire, 79–84, 105
  acquittal of, 29–30, 110–11, 113
  additional charges against, 30
  antiunion position, 12
  bail paid by, 28
  business practices, 2, 4, 6
  chronology, 122–24
  civil rights suit, 30
  evidence against, 27–28
  on fire origins, 82–83
  indictment of, 85, 108–9
  indifference of, 27
  insurance coverage, 39
  insurance money collected by, 30
  lawsuits against, 112–13
  new shirtwaist factory, 27
  photograph, 7*f*
  public demand for punishment of, 27–28,
    112–13
  roof escape, 17, 81–82, 104

  supervision by, 11
  trial of, 28–29
  Triangle Waist Company strike and, 59
  wealth of, 5
hats, of women workers, 6, 10, 15, 57
Heimsblot, Alice, 68
high-rise factories, 39–42
Holt, Hamilton, 50, 51, 85
housing, for immigrant workers, 53

immigrant women workers. *See also* Italian
    immigrant workers; Jewish immigrant
    workers; women workers
  clothing of, 55
  contractors and, 6
  education of, 54–55
  housing for, 53
  industrialization and, 1
  labor unions and, 2, 63–65
  romantic relationships, 53, 54, 55
  Russian Jewish, 56–57
  Sabbath and, 8, 52
  socialism and, 3
  strikes and, 66–68
  in sweatshops, 46–50, 50–55
  treatment of, 57
  unification of, 15
  union membership and, 64–65
Independent, The, 50, 51
"Indictments in the Asch Fire Case" (*The
    Outlook*), 108–9
industrial accidents, 2, 32, 33
  annual, 107
  fatal, 107
  in sweatshops, 54
  Triangle Waist Company, 4
  workman's compensation for, 121
industrialization
  immigrant women and, 1
  Progressive reformers and, 2–3
  regulation of factories, 32
  social change and, 2
  sweatshops, 2
  working conditions and, 14
"influential women," 97
"inside shops," 5
insurance coverage, 27, 40, 84
International Ladies Garment Workers
    Union (ILGWU), 11–12, 84
  chronology, 122–24
  fire investigations and, 27
  garment industry and, 12–13
  growth of, 71
  Local 25, 56
  memorial for unidentifiable victims,
    23, 123
  Newman, Pauline, and, 21–22
  relief drive, 25
  Schneiderman, Rose, and, 99
  Triangle Waist Company strike and, 12, 16

Italian immigrant workers. *See also* immigrant women workers; women workers
  fire victims, 92–93, 109
  garment industry and, 8
  Jewish immigrant workers and, 15, 70

Jewish immigrant workers. *See also* immigrant women workers; women workers
  fire victims, 84–87, 91–93
  garment industry and, 8
  Italian immigrant workers and, 15, 70
  Polish, 66
  reformers and, 3–4
  Russian, 56–57, 63
  Sabbath and, 8
  sewing and, 8
  socialism and, 3
  women and girls, 8
  working conditions, 56–57
Joint Relief Committee, 94, 96
jumping deaths, 18, 33, 72–75, 85–86, 102–3, 117
  firefighters and, 19*f*
  newspaper accounts of, 76–79

Labor Department, New York City, 118
labor movement
  growth of, 71
  immigrant women and, 2
  Triangle Waist Factory fire and, 33
labor unions
  arrests and, 16, 58–61, 67–68
  garment industry and, 6
  Great Hall, Cooper Union, meeting, 12–13
  growth of, 71
  immigrant women workers and, 63–65
  Lemlich, Clara, and, 63–65
  lockouts and, 67
  membership in, 64–65
  recognition of, 69
  risks of joining, 12
  strikers, 13*f*
  Triangle Waist Company fire and, 106–7
  Triangle Waist Company opposition to, 4, 12, 16, 86–87, 104–5
  Triangle Waist Company strike and, 12–13
Ladies' Waist and Dressmakers' Union, 94, 106
laundry workers' strike, 98
Lehan, Jimmy, 76–77
Lemlich, Clara, 11, 31, 114
  beating of, 12
  factory investigation by, 31
  labor union development and, 63–65
  "Life in the Shop," 56–57
  on Triangle Waist Company strike, 25
  Triangle Waist Company strike and, 12–13, 15
Life and Labor, 94

"Life in the Shop" (Lemlich), 56–57
"lifelets," 50
Lipschitz, Diana, 81
Literary Digest, 28
  "147 Dead, Nobody Guilty," 110–11
locked doors, 17, 18, 28, 29, 30, 32, 79, 83, 85, 103–5, 112–13, 117, 124
  indictments and, 108–9
lockouts
  Triangle Waist Company, 59
  union membership and, 67
loft buildings. *See also* shirtwaist factories
  defined, 5
  description, 40
  elevators, 42
  fire department protection of, 41
  fire escapes for, 41
  fireproof, 40–41
  flammable materials in, 42
  inappropriate for factories, 40–41
  insurance for, 40
  narrow passageways and, 42
  in New York City, 39–42
  sewing machine arrangement in, 41
  stairways, 42
  working conditions, 41
Lower East Side, 22–23, 25

magistrates, 14–15
Mailly, William
  "Working Girls' Strike, The," 69–70
male workers
  control of earnings by, 10
  strikes and, 70
Maltese, Salvatore, 16
Maltese, Sara, 16
Marot, Helen, 61, 88
mass production
  in garment industry, 5
  in Triangle Shirtwaist Company, 5–6
McClure's Magazine, 39
McFarlane, Arthur E.
  "Fire and the Skyscraper: The Problem of Protecting Workers in New York's Tower Factories," 39–42
media. *See* newspapers
Metropolitan Opera House meeting, 117–18, 123
  Committee of Safety and, 30
  Rose Schneiderman's speech at, 26, 99–101, 107
middle-class reformers, 3–4, 14
"mink brigade," 14, 66
Morgan, Anne, 65, 99
Morgan, J. Pierpont, 65
Morgenthau, Henry, 30, 31
morgue, 22*f*, 86, 104
Moskowitz, Henry, 117–18
muckraking journals, 39
Munsey, Frank, 62
Munsey's Magazine, 61–62

National Park Service, 124
neckwear makers' strike, 98
Newman, Pauline, 6, 8, 31, 114, 119
   depression following fire, 21–22
   factory investigation by, 31
   reform efforts, 11
newspapers
   accounts of Triangle Waist Building fire
     in, 72–79
   political cartoons and editorials, 26–27
   strike coverage, 15
New York *Call*, 111
New York City
   Building Department, 26, 84, 105
   Democratic political machine, 3
   fire department, 1, 17–21, 19*f*, 21*f*, 41
   high-rise factories, 39–42
   Labor Department, 118
   shirtwaist factories, 6
New York City Citizens Committee on
   Safety, 99
New York School of Philanthropy, 43
New York state legislature, 32
New York Times, 14–15, 24, 28, 99,
   100–101, 110
   "Arrest Strikers for Being Assaulted,"
     58–61
   "Church to the Aid of Girl Workers,"
     66–68
   "120,000 Pay Tribute to the Fire Victims,"
     87–90
   "Partners' Account of the Disaster," 79–84
New York Tribune, 28, 110–11
New York World
   "The Triangle Fire," 72–75

"147 Dead, Nobody Guilty" (*Literary
   Digest*), 110–11
"120,000 Pay Tribute to the Fire Victims"
   (*New York Times*), 87–90
open shops, 86
Outlook, The
   "Indictments in the Asch Fire Case,"
     108–9
"Out of the Shadow" (Cohen), 46–50
overtime, 87

panic, 17, 29–30, 80–81
"Partners' Account of the Disaster" (*New
   York Times*), 79–84
partnership (group) system, 44
part-time work, 45
patrol wagons, 75
Perkins, Frances, 31, 33, 99, 114, 124
   "Roosevelt I Knew, The," 119–21
picket lines, 97
piece work
   in garment industry, 8, 56
   salary work versus, 49
pin money, 97
pogroms, 91, 91*n*1

police
   support of employers by, 59
   Triangle Waist Company fire and, 1, 21*f*,
     76–77, 102–3
   Triangle Waist Company strike and,
     14–15, 59, 60, 97, 102
Polish Jewish immigrants, 66
poverty, 10
"Preliminary Report of the Factory
   Investigating Commission" (State
   of New York), 114–16
price scales, in shirtwaist factories, 45–46
Progressive reformers
   Factory Investigating Committee and,
     117
   factory reforms, 123
   garment industry and, 3, 11, 14
   industrialization and, 2–3
   Jewish immigrants and, 3–4
   middle-class reformers, 3–4, 14
   muckraking journals, 39
   shirtwaist factories and, 43–46
   social change and, 3–4
   social class and, 3–4, 14, 97
   Tammany Hall and, 32
   women workers and, 14
prosecution witnesses, 29
Protocol of Peace, 30–31, 108

Red Cross
   dependency concerns, 25
   Emergency Relief Committee, 90–93,
     94–95, 95*n*1, 98*n*7, 99, 106
   relief funds, 25, 90–93, 94, 106, 123
reform movements. *See* Progressive
   reformers
relief funds, 90–93, 94, 95, 95*n*1, 105
Report of the Red Cross Emergency Relief
   Committee of the Charity Organization
   of the Society of the City of New York,
   90–93
Robins, Margaret Dreier (Mrs. Raymond),
   15, 58, 89
romantic relationships, 53, 54, 55
roof escape, 17, 18, 80–82, 104
Roosevelt, Eleanor, 124
Roosevelt, Franklin D., 31, 33, 119
"Roosevelt I Knew, The" (Perkins), 119–21
Rosen, Annie, 86
Rosenfeld, Morris, 23*f*
Rubin, Ruth, 23*f*
Russian Jewish immigrants, 56–57, 63. *See
   also* Jewish immigrant workers
   fire victims, 91–93

Sabbath, 8, 52
Safran, Rosey
   "Washington Place Fire, The," 84–87
salary work
   in garment industry, 56
   piece work vs., 49

Salemi, Sophie, 22
Schiff, Jacob, 99
Schneiderman, Rose, 16, 23, 25, 31, 66–67,
   88, 114, 119, 123, 124
   "All for One," 99–101
   factory investigation by, 31
   Metropolitan Opera House speech, 26,
      99–101, 107
Schwartz, Margaret, 28
sewing, Jewish immigrants and, 8
sewing machines
   arrangement of, in loft factories, 41
   arrangement of, in new factory,
      27–28
   arrangement of, in Triangle Waist
      Company, 5, 18
   mass production and, 5
Shepherd, William, 72
shirtwaist factories, 6. *See also* loft
      buildings; sweatshops; Triangle
      Waist Company
   business side of, 43–44
   child labor in, 49
   contracting system in, 44
   economic cycle, 6
   employment in, 6
   feller hands, 46–50
   fireproof, 40–41, 74
   flammable materials in, 42, 74
   floor space arrangement in, 41, 42
   inspection of, 117–19
   loft buildings for, 39–42
   narrow passageways in, 42
   number of, 6, 43
   partnership or group system, 44
   price scales, 45–46
   Progressive reformers and, 43–46
   seasonality of, 45, 69, 95
   strikes in, 62–65
   sweatshops, 46–50
   training, 44
   wages, 45, 49, 69
   work-force reductions, 45
   working conditions, 31, 56–57, 69, 119
   working hours, 69
shirtwaists
   defined, 2
   fashion trends, 6, 9–10
   mass production of, 5
   popularity of, 5
   prices of, 5
"Shirtwaist Trade, The" (Goodman and
      Ueland), 43–46
shoes, of women workers, 57
"silent parade," 90
skirts, 5
skyscrapers, factories in, 39–42
slums, 2
Smith, Alfred E., 31, 32, 119, 120
   "Up to Now: An Autobiography,"
      117–19

social change, 2, 3–4
social class
   clothing and, 6, 10
   reform movements and, 3–4, 14, 97
Socialism and Socialist party, 32, 56, 66,
      69, 89
   goals of, 3
   Newman, Pauline, and, 11
   strikes and, 61
   supporters of, 3
   trade unionists, 10–11
   Triangle Waist Company strike
      and, 16
social justice, 4, 15
sprinkler systems, 105, 117
stairways, 27, 42
State of New York
   "Preliminary Report of the Factory
      Investigating Commission,"
      114–16
Stein, Leon, 112
Steuer, Max, 28–29
"Story of a Sweatshop Girl, The" (Frowne),
      50–55
strikebreakers, 12, 58, 59–60
strikers
   arrests of, 16, 58–61, 67, 102
   fines assessed against, 15, 97
   punishment of, 15
   treatment of, 14–15
strikes. *See also* Triangle Waist Company
      strike
   garment industry, 15–16, 55, 56
   male workers and, 70
   as men's weapon, 65
   Protocol of Peace and, 30–31
   in shirtwaist factories, 62–65
   Socialism and, 62
   Triangle Waist Company, 12–16
   women's use of, 65
subcontracting. *See* contracting system
suffragists/suffragettes, 89
Survey, The, 32
"sweating," 2, 5, 97
sweatshops. *See also* shirtwaist factories
   industrial accidents in, 54
   unsanitary nature of, 57
   wages, 52, 55
   women workers, 50–55
   working conditions in, 2, 46–50
   working hours, 48–49, 52, 54

Tammany Hall, 31
   antireform attitudes, 4
   progressive reform and, 32
   protection of employers by, 3
"Tammany Twins," 117
tarpaulins, 78. *See also* fire nets
theater, 9, 55
"The Triangle Fire" (*The New York World*),
      72–75

"Thrilling Incidents in Gotham Holocaust
That Wiped Out One Hundred and
Fifty Lives" (*Chicago Sunday Tribune*),
76–79
"Triangle Fire, The" (Bruere), 101–7
Triangle Waist Company. *See also* Asch
Building; shirtwaist factories
antiunion position, 4, 12, 16, 84, 86–87,
104–5
Asch Building factory, 2
attempts to pit immigrants against each
other, 15
building inspections, 27, 82, 84, 105–6
child employment at, 6
chronology, 122–24
closing of, 30, 124
contracting system, 6, 11, 97
economic cycle, 6
establishment of, 7f
fire alarm boxes, 83
fire drills, 122
fire extinguishers, 105
flammable materials in, 42, 82
growth of, 5
industrial accidents, 4
as "inside shop" or "loft" industry, 5
insurance coverage, 27, 39, 84
insurance money collected by, 30, 112
lockouts, 59
mass production methods, 5–6
overtime, 87
persons employed in, 73
production, 5
profits in, 6
public animosity toward, 25
sewing machine arrangement, 5, 18
sprinkler systems, 105, 117
"sweating" by, 5
targeted by WTUL, 4
violations of workplace regulations,
112–13
wages, 87
worker theft precautions, 104–5,
112–13
working conditions, 4, 9, 11, 31, 87
working hours, 87
Triangle Waist Company fire, 16–26
acquittals, 29–30, 110–11
ambulances, 72, 78
antiunion position and, 86–87
blocked escape routes and, 18
bodies of victims, 20, 21f
burned victims, 18
causes of, 16–17
coffins for victims of, 22f, 75, 78–79
deaths, 1, 4, 16, 18–20, 23f, 72–75, 76–79,
84–87, 110–11, 112–13, 123, 124
eighth floor, 17–18, 73, 85, 86
elevators, 17, 18, 73, 78, 80, 81, 83, 104
escape from, 84–87, 104
fire buckets, 83

fire escapes, 18, 20, 41, 73–74, 83,
86, 105
firefighters, 1, 17–21, 19f, 21f
fire hoses, 19f, 20, 27
fire ladders, 1, 103
fire lines, 103
fire nets, 1, 18, 103
freight elevators, 83
funeral for unidentified victims,
23, 24f, 101
grieving friends and family, 23f
impacts of, 4, 24–25, 30–33
indictments in, 85, 108–9
investigations into, 26–33
jumping deaths, 18, 33, 72–75, 76–79,
85–86, 102–3, 117
labor reforms and, 33
labor unions and, 106–7
labor uprising, 1
lawsuits following, 112–13
locked doors and, 17, 18, 28, 29, 79, 83,
85, 103–5, 108–9, 112–13, 117, 124
memorial for victims, 23f, 123
Metropolitan Opera House meeting and,
100–101
municipal resources required for, 21
narrow passageways and, 42
newspaper accounts of, 72–79
news report of, 72–75
ninth floor, 17–18, 85, 86
origins of, 82–83, 117
outbreak of, 1, 16, 18, 85, 123
panic among workers, 17, 29–30, 80–81
police, 1, 102–3
popular interest in, 76
public accountability for, 26–27
Red Cross emergency relief funds,
90–93
relief drives, 25
relief funds to victims' families,
90–93, 105
roof escape, 17, 18, 80–82
sensational coverage of, 76
spread of, 17, 85
tarpaulins, 78
temporary morgue, 22f
tenth floor, 17–18, 85
unidentifiable victims, 20, 23, 87–90,
101, 123
women employees, 1–2
youngest victim, 16
Triangle Waist Company fire trial, 28–30
Triangle Waist Company strike, 11–16,
96n3, 97
arrests of strikers, 58–61, 102
city response to, 14–15
criticism of, 25
fire and, 86–87
ILGWU and, 12
impacts of, 15–16
media coverage of, 15

Triangle Waist Company strike (*cont.*)
  Metropolitan Opera House meeting and,
    100–101
  police and, 59, 60, 97, 102
  significance of, 70
  Socialist press and, 16
  strikebreakers, 12, 58, 59–60
  strike purposes, 12, 14, 69–70
  strikers, 13*f*
  WTUL and, 12
"Two Orphans, The," 54

Ueland, Elsa, 43
Ueland, Elsa and Pearl Goodman
  "Shirtwaist Trade, The," 43–46
underskirts, 53
United Brotherhood of Garment
  Workers, 55
United Hebrew Charities, 91, 92, 93
United Press agency, 72
"Uprising of the Twenty Thousands, The,"
  11–16, 71
"Up to Now: An Autobiography" (Smith),
  117–19
urban issues, 3

wages
  garment industry, 8, 55, 56, 57
  piece work vs. weekly employment, 49
  shirtwaist factories, 45, 69
  sweatshops, 52, 55
  Triangle Waist Company, 87
  of women workers, 11
Wagner, Robert F., 31, 32, 117, 118,
  119, 120
Walla, Anna, 59
"Washington Place Fire, The" (Safran),
  84–87
Waverly Place factory, 81, 82, 83
Weiner, Lillian, 29
"What the Grave Covers" (*Chicago Daily
  Tribune*), 112–13
Whitman, Charles, 27–28, 108–9, 110
Woman Voter, The, 94
"Women in a Labor War: How the Working
  Girls of New York East Side Have
  Learned to Use Men's Weapons in a
  Struggle for Better Conditions"
  (Benson), 61–65
women reformers
  Factory Investigation Commission
    and, 114
  middle class, 14
  motivations of, 3–4, 14
  upper class, 14, 97
  women workers and, 14
Women's Trade Union League (WTUL), 4,
  32, 66, 88, 94, 101–7, 106
  chronology, 122–23
  fire investigations and, 27

ILGWU and, 11
  strike arrests, 58–61
  strikes and, 68
  Triangle Waist Company fire and, 30
  Triangle Waist Company strike and, 12,
    15, 16
  Triangle Waist Company targeted
    by, 4
  working women and, 98
women workers. *See also* immigrant
    women workers
  attempt to discredit, 28–29
  average age of, 96
  camaraderie among, 9, 15
  compared to slaves, 8–9, 14
  contracting system and, 11
  economic issues, 94–98
  enjoyment of work by, 9
  fines assessed against, 8, 9, 11
  in garment industry, 6, 8–9
  harassment of, 9, 11
  hats, 6, 10, 15, 57
  housing for, 53
  immigrants, 1–2
  media portrayal of, 15
  militancy among, 14
  needles and thread provided by, 11
  poverty of, 10
  qualities of, 97
  reform movements and, 3–4, 14
  relief payments, 92–93
  shirtwaists (blouses) and, 2
  shoes of, 57
  social controls on, 10
  Socialist trade unionists and, 10–11
  solidarity among, 24
  strikers, 13*f*, 62–65
  support of families by, 10, 25,
    95–97, 98
  in sweatshops, 50–55
  testimony before Factory Investigating
    Commission, 114–18
  training of, 44
  treatment of, 57
  unification of, 15
  wages, 11
  women reformers and, 14
  working conditions, 2, 8–9, 10, 119
  working hours for, 121
wooden staircases, 27
worker theft precautions, 104–5
working conditions
  investigation of, 31–32, 119–21
  in loft buildings, 41
  in shirtwaist factories, 56–57, 69, 119
  in sweatshops, 46–50
  Triangle Waist Company, 4, 9, 11,
    31, 87
  women workers, 119
  for young women, 10

"Working Girls' Strike, The" (Mailly),
    69–70
working hours
    in garment industry, 55
    Sabbath and, 52
    shirtwaist factories, 69
    sweatshops, 52, 54

Triangle Waist Company, 87
    for women, 121
    work day, 121
workmen's compensation, 121
Worth, Battalion Chief, 103
WTUL. *See* Women's Trade Union League
    (WTUL)